THE CURIOUS MYSTERIES OF
ELI MARKS

The Young Eli Marks Mystery Series
(Book 1)

JOHN GASPARD

ALBERT'S BRIDGE
BOOKS

The Curious Mysteries of Eli Marks

The Young Eli Marks Mystery Series (Book 1)

First Edition | 2023

Albert's Bridge Books

The book's cover was created with MidJourney (free version) with adjustments added by the designer via PhotoShop.

ACKNOWLEDGMENTS

Special thanks to Richard Kaufman, David Parr, Tyler Erickson and Ever Elizalde for their help in bringing *Harry's Magic Emporium* tricks to life.

For Scarlet and Lydia.
Thanks for your willingness to take the first look.

CONTENTS

THE CURIOUS MYSTERIES OF ELI MARKS

TEN CURIOUS MYSTERIES FOR YOU TO SOLVE

HARRY'S MAGIC EMPORIUM

TEN FUN MAGIC TRICKS FOR YOU TO LEARN

THE CURIOUS MYSTERIES OF ELI MARKS

TEN CURIOUS MYSTERIES
FOR YOU TO SOLVE

CHAPTER ONE

THE RED-HERRING LEAGUE

IT WAS ONLY Day Two at this new school. And this was already my second visit to the principal's office.

I might have been on my way to setting some sort of record.

My first visit to the principal's office—yesterday—had been mostly social; just a quick pop-in with the Guidance Counselor. She'd been the person to sign me up for school when my Aunt Alice had brought me in. And the Guidance Counselor had then helped me locate my locker and given me a quick tour of the school.

That tour had included meeting the principal, Mr. Moore, as well as my Home Room teacher.

This special treatment was probably because I was

starting at Susan B. Anthony Middle School in mid-October. I doubt they rolled out this red-carpet treatment for every new kid.

That would be insane.

However, I wasn't the only student waiting to see Principal Moore.

Another kid about my age was seated across from me. He seemed way too relaxed for someone who was waiting to see the principal. I got the sense that he was something of a regular.

He was watching me. To be more specific, he was watching my hands.

"What are you doing?"

He spoke very slowly, like he was choosing each word with great care.

I looked down at my hands. I had forgotten I was doing it.

"It's called The French Drop," I said. "It's a magic move."

"How do you mean?"

I held out my hands to demonstrate.

"The idea is, I make this coin vanish, right before your eyes."

I held up a quarter in my left hand between my thumb and first finger. I passed my right hand over it, appearing to grab the coin. I rubbed the fingers of my right hand, finally opening that hand to show it was empty.

"Impressive," he said slowly.

I continued the short routine, taking the fingers of my left hand and appearing to pull the coin out of the fabric of my pants, right where my leg bent at the knee. I held up the newly revealed coin.

"Very nice," he added. He didn't smile and his face didn't light up. So I took him at his word that he had enjoyed the trick. "Did you get sent up here for doing magic during class?"

I shook my head. "No, I got sent up here because I kept dropping the coin while practicing. Like a lot."

He nodded. "That'll do it. You need to get quieter coins."

Before I could respond, the door to the principal's office swung open and Mr. Moore stepped out. He looked weary.

He squinted at me, then turned to the kid across from me.

"Nathan, I am surprised to see you back here so soon."

"You and me both."

"What brings you up here this morning? Shouldn't you be in science class?"

"I should be. But the substitute teacher asked me to leave."

"And the reason for that was?"

Nathan sighed deeply. "She was talking about light. She said mirrors reflect light, which is why we can see ourselves in mirrors."

"So far so good," the principal agreed.

"Then she said that mirrors are the <u>only</u> things that reflect light. I raised my hand and pointed out that <u>everything</u> reflects light. Otherwise, we couldn't see anything at all."

The principal stared at him for a long moment.

"And that's why she sent you up here?"

Nathan shrugged. "Officially, she sent me up here for talking out of turn. But I didn't talk out of turn. I raised my hand."

The principal sighed. "Okay. Do me a favor, Nathan. Talk less. Raise your hand less." He turned to me. Something about me must have puzzled him. "Didn't I just meet you? Yesterday?"

He seemed to be thinking hard about it. I saw him glance over at the woman who ran the front desk.

Then I saw her slowly and deliberately mouth two words: "Dead parents."

And Mr. Moore's mood shifted instantly. He didn't smile, but he came close. "Eli, isn't it?"

"Yes."

"And to what do I owe the pleasure of this encounter?"

"He keeps dropping his coin," Nathan offered from his chair.

I nodded as I held up the quarter. "I've been trying to learn this magic trick and I keep dropping the coin." I did a very quick version of the move. And, of course, once again I dropped the coin.

"A magic trick?" Mr. Moore repeated, turning it into a question. "Oh yes. Your guardian, your uncle, he's a magician, right?"

I nodded as I bent down to pick up the quarter. Mr. Moore thought for several seconds.

"You should get quieter coins," Mr. Moore finally said.

"I had the same suggestion," Nathan said.

"Let's do this," Mr. Moore said, ignoring Nathan's comment. "How about you save the magic practice until after school or at lunch?" He glanced up at the oversized clock on the wall. "Which is where you both should be right now. I'll walk you downstairs to the lunchroom."

He gestured for us to get up and we followed him out of the office.

THE THREE OF US DIDN'T SAY MUCH AS WE walked down the hall together. I mean, what was there to say? I didn't know this Nathan kid. And Mr. Moore didn't have a whole lot in common with a couple of thirteen-year-olds.

The hall was empty. Everyone was at lunch.

The awkward silence was broken by a shrill voice coming from a classroom as we passed it.

"Mr. Moore. Mr. Moore, I was just coming to see you."

I recognized the older woman as my new history teacher. I'd only been in the class once so far and couldn't remember her name. Mr. Moore, obviously, didn't have that problem.

"Mrs. Sorenson, what can I do for you?"

"I think someone stole the questions for my Friday history test."

This statement was serious enough to cause Mr. Moore to come to a complete stop. Nathan and I stopped as well.

"What do you mean?"

Mrs. Sorenson seemed a little breathless. But she had seemed breathless in class, so maybe that was just her normal state.

"I was upstairs, on the third floor, in the Teacher's Lounge. I had all the materials for Friday's test laid out, including the two essay questions. You see, I've given the kids fifteen possible topics for that essay, but no one knows what the actual two questions will be."

"I see," Mr. Moore said, nodding patiently. I think he wanted Mrs. Sorenson to get to the point. I sure did.

"I went into the Teacher's bathroom for a minute, and when I came out, I saw a boy rushing out of the room. He had been looking at the two essay questions, I'm sure of it. I raced to the door, but by the time I got there, he was way ahead of me, far down the hall. He turned the corner and disappeared."

I had trouble imagining Mrs. Sorenson racing anywhere. I think a quick stroll might have winded her.

"And he took the questions?" Mr. Moore asked.

Mrs. Sorenson shook her head. "He didn't need to take them. Just knowing what the two essay questions are will be a huge advantage for anyone taking the test. That would give them two days to really read up on those two topics."

"Can you describe the kid?"

Mrs. Sorenson considered this seriously for a long moment. "Not really. It all happened so quickly. But I know this much for sure: He was wearing a light shirt. And our culprit had red hair. Bright red hair."

"That certainly narrows down the suspects," Mr. Moore said.

Armed with this information, we followed Mr. Moore down one flight of stairs to the school's lower level. We made a sharp left, which took us into the lunchroom. The room was swarming with kids. Some were going through the lunch line, putting their selected food items on the trays. But most were seated at the many long tables, eating, and laughing and joking.

I didn't recognize even one face.

For the first time, it really hit me just how new to this school I was.

The only kid whose name I knew was standing right next to me. There are many reasons why Nathan went on to become my best friend, but that was certainly the first.

Mr. Moore had signaled the Room Monitor the moment he came in, and she had scurried over to him. He said a few words to her, drowned out by the din in the room. He pointed at three parts of the lunchroom, and she had raced away.

Less than a minute later, she escorted the only three red-headed boys in light shirts in the room over to Mr. Moore. He gestured them to follow him into the hallway. Since he hadn't officially released Nathan or me, we naturally tagged along as well.

As the three kids lined up in front of Mr. Moore, I got my first real look at them.

They all had red hair and wore light colored shirts, but the similarities stopped right there.

One kid was skinny and looked damp. He had clearly recently been sweating.

The second one wasn't sweating. Just the opposite. Even though he had just been called in front of the principal, he didn't show any sign of nervousness. He was what my Aunt Alice would have called a cool cucumber.

The third kid was both a little taller and a little wider than the other two. To my eyes, he looked too big to still be in middle school. I don't know which team he was on, but he clearly played sports of some kind. He may have constituted a whole team all by himself.

Looking at these three students, it occurred to me I was looking at the school's social structure, broken down into just three people: The nerd, the cool guy and the jock.

For his part, Mr. Moore didn't waste any time.

"We've just come from Mrs. Sorenson's classroom. Someone with red hair and a light-colored shirt was spotted stealing a look at the essay questions for her Friday history test. Where have you each been for the last fifteen minutes?"

The question was addressed to all three boys, but Mr. Moore turned to the sweating kid first. Probably because he was sweating.

"Ronald?"

The kid looked not only damp but also terrified. "I just got here a couple minutes ago. Coach made me swim some extra laps after swim class. He said I was horsing around too much. I got my lunch and sat down over there." He pointed across the room. "They were out of pizza by the time I got here. So instead, I got stuck with yesterday's mystery meat."

He didn't appear to be lying. There was an empty chair where he pointed. A plate of something resembling a brownish substance was awaiting the return of its owner.

"Extra laps?" Mr. Moore repeated. "So, you're not sweating from running?"

"I <u>am</u> sweating from running," Ronald agreed.

"But I'm also still wet from the pool and the quick shower. I wanted to get here before they ran out of pizza."

"How are you doing in Mrs. Sorenson's history class?"

Ronald shrugged. "About the same as every other class. Getting by."

"I see." Mr. Moore turned to the kid in the middle, who was smirking at Ronald's lament about the pizza.

"Simon?"

"Been here the whole lunch hour," Simon said with a confident grin. "You can ask the guys at my table." He gestured toward a nearby table, which was filled with boys who all appeared to be variations on Simon. They were all smirking back at us. "I went to the bathroom for like two minutes, but I didn't go anywhere near the third floor. The guys will back me up on that."

"And how are you doing in history class?"

"I get good grades in all my classes. I don't need to cheat."

Mr. Moore thought about this and then turned to the third kid.

"What about you Bob?"

"I was eating lunch," the big kid said. "I had finished my first round and went back for seconds." He turned and gave a wicked smile at the skinny kid. "And I got the last couple pieces of pizza. The lunch ladies saw me. They can back me up."

"But you've had some trouble in that class before, haven't you?"

Bob shrugged. "I'm behind on my reading. But I'll pass the test, no problem."

"I see," Mr. Moore said slowly as he stared at the red-headed trio. He pursed his lips. Finally, he made a decision.

"Well, despite Mrs. Sorenson seeing a student with red hair running away, I don't think I'm in a position to pin this particular offense on any one of you three."

"Actually, Mr. Moore," I said. "I think it's pretty clear which one of these kids stole a peek at the essay questions."

The principal stared down at me, a look of surprise on his face. I think he may have even forgotten I was still there.

"Really? How do you figure, Eli?"

HOW DID ELI KNOW WHICH ONE OF THE BOYS HAD PEEKED AT THE QUESTIONS?

"Mrs. Sorenson's history classroom is one floor up, on the second floor," I said. "Which is where anyone would naturally assume the test questions would be: In her classroom. But Mrs. Sorenson told us that the mystery kid saw the questions while she was in the Teachers' Lounge, which is one floor higher. The third floor."

I turned to Simon. I could tell he was beginning to seethe but doing his best to hide it.

"He said he hasn't been on the <u>third floor</u> all day," I continued. "But you'd only mention the third floor if you'd been there and seen the questions. Otherwise, you'd say you hadn't been on the <u>second floor</u>, near Mrs. Sorenson's classroom. Which is where you'd naturally assume the questions were."

The principal considered this for a long moment. "You make a good point, Eli. Unfortunately, there's really no way to prove it, one way or the other."

"That's right," Simon said quickly. "There's no way to prove it."

"It's a bit of a conundrum," Mr. Moore said.

"Not really," I said. "The simplest solution is for Mrs. Sorenson to pick two different topics for the essay questions. Then it doesn't matter if anyone—including this guy—saw the questions ahead of time."

"Good thought," Mr. Moore agreed. "Thank you, Eli. You can all return to your lunches."

With that he turned and left the lunchroom, probably on his way to deal with yet another crisis.

Simon sneered at me as he returned to his lunch table. He shifted his sneer to a self-confident smile as he sat down with his laughing friends.

For his part, Nathan seemed delighted at the outcome of the encounter. I mean, as delighted as he ever seemed to get about anything.

"That was some slick thinking, Eli," he said.

"Thanks."

"So, you want to show me how you do that French Drop thing again? Spend lunch dropping a few coins together?"

"Sure thing," I said as we headed toward the other side of the bustling room. I was hoping there was still something edible in the lunch line.

To be honest, I was still a little stunned.

In the course of about twenty minutes, I had solved a mystery and found a brand-new friend.

Not bad for Day Two at a new school.

CHAPTER TWO
"A" IS FOR APPENDIX

HOW MANY THIRTEEN-YEAR-OLD kids do you know who have their own apartment?

None?

Well now you do.

How I ended up in my own apartment above a magic shop in South Minneapolis is a bit of a tale.

The short version is this: my parents died, and I was taken in by my Aunt Alice and Uncle Harry. They were older than my parents (like, by a lot) and they didn't have any kids of their own. But what they did have was a magic shop with a one-bedroom apartment right above it.

The problem? That's where they lived. Which meant there wasn't really room for me.

However, they also had *another* one-bedroom

apartment, one floor above theirs (and two floors up from the magic shop).

Problem solved, right?

Sort of.

For years, Uncle Harry had used that extra apartment as his storage facility. In it he hoarded his books on magic. His old magic props. Videos of past performances. And his mammoth record collection. Plus various odds and ends he was *absolutely convinced* he would need someday.

Was there room up there for a thirteen-year-old boy?

Yes. Eventually.

After considerable re-arranging (and some grumbled arguments about finally throwing some things out), they carved out a bedroom for me.

Meals were downstairs, at their kitchen table. Evenings were spent in their living room. But when it was time to go to bed, I climbed those way-too steep stairs up to my bedroom, snaking my way through the magic museum/junk shop I called home.

Soon after I arrived, Uncle Harry set up an ancient intercom system between my bedroom and their kitchen. This allowed Aunt Alice to call me for meals without blowing out her vocal cords. Or climbing those ridiculously steep stairs.

And then, like it does, life went on.

I don't think either one of them really knew what to do with a full-time kid on the premises. Aunt Alice reacted by talking way too much. Uncle Harry went the other direction, uttering grunts more than words.

Magic was his communication method of choice.

At least for a while.

After he'd made a quarter disappear and then pulled it out from behind my ear, (for the third time) I asked him how it was done.

He sat down and taught me The French Drop. The words poured out of him. In that few minutes, it was the most he had said to me since the day I'd arrived.

I didn't realize it at the time, but magic was to become our primary method of communication for years to come.

"ELI, DINNER'S ALMOST READY."

Aunt Alice's voice crackled with static through the intercom, but it was clear enough to understand. And I was hungry. So, I headed down one flight to their apartment.

She was busy at the stove when I came in. I took

my seat at the kitchen table, glancing into the living room to check on Harvey.

Harvey was Uncle Harry's white rabbit. Harry had made the rabbit appear (and disappear) for years as part of his magic act. But now both were semi-retired.

Harvey didn't seem to mind semi-retirement. He hung out in his crate in the corner of the living room. And, when the spirit moved him, he'd hop over and look out the window. Then he'd hop back to his crate.

I don't think Uncle Harry was adjusting to semi-retirement with the same enthusiasm.

He came into the kitchen, grunted a greeting in my general direction, and then took his seat. He glanced around the room, looking at anything but me.

Then an idea must have struck him.

He dug into his pocket and took out a quarter. Then he reached over to the center of the table and grabbed the saltshaker.

He placed the quarter in the center of the table, then unrolled the cloth napkin Aunt Alice had put at each place setting.

With great care, he placed the saltshaker on top of the quarter. Then he covered the saltshaker with the napkin, encasing the shaker so tightly that I could detect its shape within the folds of the napkin.

"Did you know, Eli," he said slowly. "That even a

solid tabletop will have, from time to time, weak spots that are large enough for small objects—such as a quarter—to pass through them?"

I shook my head. He picked up the saltshaker, still draped by the napkin, as he pointed at the quarter.

"Well, we've had this table for years and years," he continued. "And I know that it has a weak spot right about here." He pushed on the coin a bit, with no results. So, he covered it again with the saltshaker hidden inside the napkin.

Then, without warning, he slammed his hand down hard on the napkin, which immediately flattened against the table.

At the same time, I heard a small *thud* from below.

Harry picked up the napkin, revealing that the quarter was still there atop the table. But the saltshaker was gone.

"Well, that wasn't the result I expected," he muttered.

I bent over in my chair and peered at the floor beneath the table.

The saltshaker lay on the rug, directly under the spot where it had been resting under the napkin moments before.

I crawled under the table and picked it up. It appeared to be a normal saltshaker in every way.

"Harry, stop playing with the food," Alice said. She sounded a little annoyed as she set a plate in front of him. She put another plate in front of me.

"I wasn't playing with the food, dear. I was playing with the condiments."

"Whatever," she mumbled as she returned to the counter to grab her own plate. And then she joined us at the table.

We sat in silence for several moments while we ate.

I had come to understand that silence was something that Aunt Alice really didn't like.

"So, I went to that new veterinarian to get Harvey's rabbit food this afternoon," she said, sort of out of the blue. "You know, the one over on Cedar Avenue?"

I didn't know, but I nodded politely. I had no idea where Cedar Avenue was.

"Anyway, I saw the cutest dog there," she continued. "The Vet was just bringing him out to the owner in the lobby. He was wearing one of those silly plastic cones around his neck."

"The veterinarian was?" Harry said.

"No, the dog," Alice said.

I think Harry had been joking and that Aunt Alice had missed the joke. I think that happened a lot.

"Anyway, it was such a cute dog, a little black Lab,

I think. According to the Vet, he's just had his appendix out."

"The Vet or the dog?" Harry asked. I think he might have winked at me as he said it.

"Well, the dog of course. So now he—the dog—must wear that silly plastic cone until his sutures are fully healed." Aunt Alice turned to me. "We always wanted a dog. But with all the touring, it just wasn't possible. And now, living above the magic shop. Well, there's no backyard. Just not a good place for a dog, sadly."

As I understood it, Alice had toured with Harry for years as his magic assistant. I'd seen a couple of framed posters of the two of them on the wall in my apartment upstairs. At least I think it was Harry and Alice. In the posters, they were a lot younger.

"This Vet was so nice and affable. As soon as he was done with the dog owner, a woman came up to him with a big shoebox. Didn't have an appointment, wasn't standing in line like I was. Just got right in his face and said, 'My son found this snake and wants to keep it. Is it safe? Is it going to hurt him?'"

Alice shook her head and clucked her tongue.

"So rude," she continued. "But he was nice to her, nicer than I might have been. He looked into the box, glanced at the snake and said, 'Not to worry, it's safe.

It's not a poisonous snake.'" And without so much as a 'thank you,' the woman left."

"People," Harry grumbled.

"Indeed," Alice agreed. "But anyway, here's the point of my story: I finally got up to the counter and asked to buy a bag of Harvey's rabbit food. And before the young woman could go get it, this nice veterinarian stopped in mid-step and came over. He asked how old Harvey is, and I told him. And he suggested a different food for Harvey. He explained that it's a bit more expensive, but that it keeps older rabbits from regurgitating their food. So, I bought that one instead. I was really impressed with that veterinarian and the way he deals with clients. Very much a people person."

Harry and I started to speak at the same time.

He gestured for me to go first.

"I was just going to say," I began. "That he might be good with people, but you'd have to be crazy to ever go back to him again. He's not good at his job."

Harry nodded. "I was going to use a stronger term," he said. He looked across the table at me. "Eli, what one thing made you say that about him?"

WHY DOES ELI QUESTION THE SKILLS OF THIS VETERINARIAN?

"It was more than one thing," I said. "In fact, it was virtually <u>everything</u>. To begin with, dogs don't have appendixes. So, I don't know what he removed from that dog—if he did anything more than just cut him enough to need sutures—but it wasn't an appendix."

"Really?" Aunt Alice said slowly. She looked over at Harry, who nodded in agreement.

"The second thing is, I think he's ripping you off by selling you that higher-priced rabbit food. Because rabbits can't throw-up." Aunt Alice winced. I don't think she liked that term.

"They can't regurgitate," I said. "That's not how their digestive systems work."

"Goodness," she said softly.

"And finally, maybe I'm just picking nits, but when it comes to the snake, he used the wrong word. He should have told her it wasn't <u>venomous</u>. Venomous means the snake would inject you with toxins when it bites you."

Harry was still nodding. "A poisonous snake is one that will poison you if you <u>eat</u> it. Very few snakes are poisonous," he added.

"Anyway, I wouldn't go back there if I were you," I said. I returned my attention back to my food.

"Well then I won't," Alice said quickly. "But right after dinner, I am going to write him a very strong letter."

"While you do that," Harry suggested, "Eli, do you want me to show you how the saltshaker trick works?"

I don't know how much fun Aunt Alice had writing her scathing letter.

But Harry and I had a great time for the next hour.

And before I knew it, I was doing the trick like a pro.

CHAPTER THREE

THE GIRL WITH THE DAI VERNON TATTOO

"I DON'T WANT TO GO." I wasn't pleading, but that would be my next step if this didn't work. "I won't know anybody."

"Well, maybe not at the start. But you're bound to meet some people your own age by the end of the meeting." Aunt Alice wasn't insisting, but I could tell that would be <u>her</u> next step.

I wisely recognized this was an argument I was not going to win. Particularly since the meeting was taking place just downstairs.

I hadn't spent a lot of time in Uncle Harry's magic shop since arriving. It's not like I had been avoiding it. But what with moving in and then starting school, I hadn't had a lot of free time during the store's business hours.

So, it was still mostly unexplored territory.

I was even more unfamiliar with the shop's back room, which was where Harry's monthly magic meeting was taking place.

It wasn't technically Harry's meeting. It was a magic club meeting for which Harry had generously offered his back room.

I stood in the doorway to the space, standing halfway in the store and halfway in the back room. In reality, I was trying to be nowhere.

The room was filled with a small crowd of about twenty-five people. Virtually all of them were men, most of them gray haired. Or well on their way to being gray haired. There were also a handful of older teens, gathered in a corner, laughing about something.

I naturally assumed they were laughing at me. But in reality, I don't think they'd given me a second look.

Surprisingly, there was one girl. She might have been close to my age. I'm not sure. She was certainly in the ballpark. She was dressed in a very funky way, including a red fedora hat on her head and bright red high-top sneakers on her feet.

Then the meeting was called to order and people took their seats in the rows of folding chairs.

An older man who had been talking to Uncle Harry must have been in charge, because he was the one who started the meeting. And he was the one who kept it moving. He wasn't kidding around. When in doubt, he consulted a paperback book in his hands, called *Robert's Rules of Order.* I don't know who this guy Robert was, but he sure had a lot of rules.

It was all very official, with a reading of the minutes of the last meeting ... a report from committee heads ... a discussion of old business ... an introduction of new business ... and then the segment that most of the group seemed to be excited about.

"Okay, this is our performance segment. Is there anyone who wants to demonstrate something you've been working on?"

Many hands shot up. The meeting's leader called people up one by one.

And that's when the evening finally got interesting.

One middle-aged man did a trick which involved cutting a piece of rope in half and then putting it back together. Even from my position in the doorway, I could see his hands were shaking. His voice wasn't doing much better. But he got through the trick and was rewarded with polite applause and words of encouragement from the group.

The next two performers—a teenager and a much older man—fared a little better. The teenager did something with billiard balls, making them appear and disappear very quickly. Maybe a little too quickly. He had brought along a boom box, which played energetic music while he performed. He tried to keep pace with the music, which wasn't helping him as much as he thought it was.

Then the older gentleman stepped forward with five large silver rings. He didn't have music. He just did a routine where he magically joined and unjoined (is that a word?) the rings, one after another. Even though I think I figured out the secret right away, it really didn't matter. He was amazing to watch.

Next up was the girl I had seen earlier. The guy in charge called her Cecilia and she walked up to the front of the room like she owned the place.

"I've been working on a little hypnotism, which I'd like to try out tonight. Do I have a volunteer?"

Several hands shot up in the air, but she ignored them and turned to me.

"Since I need a doorway for this experiment and you're already standing in a doorway, do you want to help me out?"

What choice did I have?

Cecilia walked over to me.

"Hi, I'm Cecilia."

"I'm Eli."

"Well, Eli, I've been working on learning how to hypnotize people. And I'm getting better at it. The problem is, so far, I can only hypnotize people one joint or limb at a time. Let me show you what I mean."

She instructed me to place my right foot against the door frame, with my left foot a few inches away.

Then she waved her hands in front of my left knee, saying very seriously, "You are getting sleepy. Very sleepy."

There were some snickers from the group. I was having trouble not laughing myself.

Cecilia stepped back. "All right, I think it worked. Let's test it out. Eli, do me a favor: Without moving any other muscles, lift your left leg off the floor."

I smiled at this silly request and went to lift my left leg.

It wouldn't move.

I couldn't lift my left leg off the floor.

I looked up at her for help, but she only smiled back at me. She turned to the group.

"Eli, can you lift your left leg?"

"No," I stammered. "No, I can't."

There was mild applause from the group.

"Let's see if we can wake that knee up," Cecilia said as she turned back to me. She looked down at my knee. "When I snap my fingers, you will awaken."

She snapped her fingers and then took my hand, gesturing for me to step forward. I did it, tentatively at first, finally realizing that the strength had returned to my left leg.

She held up my hand as she turned back to the crowd.

"And that, my friends, is hypnotism."

As they applauded, Cecilia turned and winked at me.

And this time, <u>both</u> my knees felt a little weak.

THE MOMENT THE MEETING'S LEADER suggested taking a break, Aunt Alice appeared, as if by magic. She carried a tray of cookies and two pitchers of lemonade.

She set them on a folding table and—just as quickly as she'd come—Alice disappeared.

"That was a good trick," I said as I nervously took another bite from a cookie.

I took a sip of the sour lemonade as Cecilia snagged a cookie of her own off the tray.

"Thanks," she said. "I still haven't decided what kind of magic I want to do. So, I'm trying out mentalism for a while."

"What's mentalism?"

She cocked her head to one side. I think she thought I was joking.

"A guy at a magic meeting who's willing to ask questions and admits to things he doesn't know? Eli, I think you're going to go far."

"Thanks. But what's mentalism?"

"It's tricks you do with people's minds, instead of with cards or coins."

"You can learn that here?"

"You would be amazed what you can learn here." She grabbed my shoulder and turned me. "You see those two guys talking to your uncle Harry?"

I looked across the room. Harry was deep in conversation with two other old men.

"Yes."

"The one on the left is Abe Ackerman. He's one of the best mentalists in the country. He taught me the knee trick. The one on the other side is Max Monarch. He does miracles with cards. Last week, he taught me how to do a second deal. Your uncle is probably more famous than both put together. Harry's done it all: kids shows, touring shows, big illusions. He's been on *The Ed Sullivan Show* like a million times."

She glanced around the room at the other small

groups of magicians. They were all chatting and demonstrating tricks for each other.

"Most of these guys have no idea how lucky they are to be right here, right now, in the same room with these masters. I can't speak for the rest of them, but I'm here to learn as much as I can."

She took a sip of lemonade. As she raised her glass, I noticed something on her arm.

"Is that a tattoo?"

She glanced down at her arm and then quickly scanned the room.

"I was wondering who would be the first one to notice," she said quietly. "You win."

I looked at the tattoo more closely. It appeared to be an older guy with a mustache.

"Who is that?"

Cecilia continued to speak quietly. "It's Dai Vernon."

"Who is that?"

"Boy, you really are a newbie, aren't you? He's a really famous guy in the magic world. They called him The Professor. He died about ten years ago, so I missed out on ever meeting him. I'm just waiting for one of these clowns to see the tattoo. They'll freak."

"Your parents let you get a tattoo?"

She shook her head. "It's actually a temporary tattoo. And to be honest, it's of Walt Disney. My dad got it for me the last time he was in California, at Disneyland. But it looks enough like Dai Vernon to fool this crowd. If anyone—besides you—ever notices."

"Eli, you are a very wise young man." This came from Uncle Harry, who had crossed the room to grab a cookie for himself. "You've picked the smartest young magician in the room to chat with."

Cecilia blushed. "Thanks, Mr. Marks."

"Don't be silly. You're one of the few magicians in this room who could benefit from a little less humility."

Before she could respond, we were interrupted by a squat, balding man. He was a little out of breath as he sidled up to Harry.

"Harry, Harry, look what Duane Hartwell is willing to sell," the man said. He was still panting from his trek across the room.

He held up a plastic sleeve, inside of which appeared to be a single, unfolded sheet of paper.

"What have we here?" Harry asked as he took the sleeve and looked at its contents.

"It's a handwritten note, from Karl Germain to Dai Vernon, complimenting him on his show. You know I collect letters between magicians and this one is a real find."

I began to think the man was panting more from excitement than from the exertion of walking across the room.

Cecilia turned to me. "Karl Germain was a magician and a mentalist. One of the best. He died years and years ago," she added.

"Duane Hartwell is willing to sell this, is he?" Harry said slowly. He glanced across the room at a small cluster of middle-aged magicians. A red-haired man seemed to be leading the conversation. He laughed, a little too loudly and a little too long at one of his own jokes.

"What do you make of this, Cecilia?" Harry asked as he handed her the plastic sleeve.

I looked over her shoulder as she glanced at the note. According to the logo at the top, it was hotel stationary from the Americana Hotel in Miami. This logo was flanked by two standard US flags. I had trouble making out the writing through the plastic, but Cecilia didn't seem to have the same issue.

"*'April 31, 1957,'*" she read. "*'Dai, just a quick note. What a wonderful show last night. One remarkable effect after another. You continue to wow me with every new routine. Let's grab lunch at The Castle next time*

I'm in town. Safe travels! Best, (signed) Karl Germain.'"

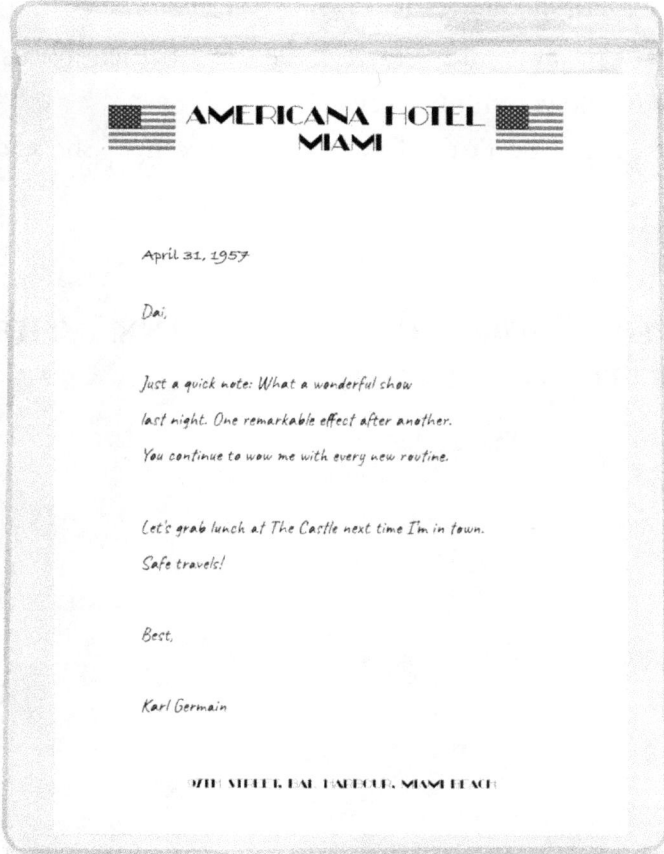

AMERICANA HOTEL MIAMI

April 31, 1957

Dai,

Just a quick note: What a wonderful show
last night. One remarkable effect after another.
You continue to wow me with every new routine.

Let's grab lunch at The Castle next time I'm in town.
Safe travels!

Best,

Karl Germain

9711 STREET, BAL HARBOUR, MIAMI BEACH

She looked up at Harry and then at the balding man.

"How much is Mr. Hartwell charging for this?" she asked.

"Only a hundred dollars," he said quickly. "What do you think, Harry? Is it a good deal?"

"I'm not sure," Harry said. He turned to us. "What do you think, Cecilia?"

"Me? I don't think it's worth two cents," she said flatly.

WHY DOES CECILIA THINK THE LETTER IS WORTHLESS?

"I TEND TO AGREE," HARRY SAID. "THIS letter is about as far from authentic as one can get." He turned to me. "Any thoughts on this one, Eli?"

Cecilia handed it to me and I looked at the note more closely. It was on an uncreased, full-sized sheet of stationary, encased in a thick plastic sleeve.

"Well," I said slowly. "The first thing I notice is that not only is the date wrong; it's impossible. There is no April 31st. April only has thirty days."

"Indeed it does," Harry agreed.

"But that's a mistake anyone could have made." I continued to look at the document. "It's also weird that this guy wrote this other guy a letter, but the paper's never been folded."

"Ah, another good point," Harry said with a chuckle. "Do you agree, Cecilia?"

"I hadn't considered that," she said. "I was too focused on the image of the US flag at the top of the stationary. The letter is dated 1957, but at that point I don't think we had 50 states yet. I don't think Hawaii and Alaska came around for a couple more years. Yet that is clearly a fifty-star flag."

"Indeed, it is," Harry said. "We didn't have a flag with fifty stars on it until at least 1960. Which puts this sheet of letterhead a bit ahead of its time, don't you think?"

He handed the plastic sleeve back to the balding man. "I'm sorry, but I think your friend Duane is taking you for a bit of a ride on this one."

The guy looked crushed. "Are you sure," he said. His voice cracked just a bit.

"Well, Eli and Cecilia both make good points," Harry said. "However, what seals the deal for me is his offer to have lunch at The Castle. One assumes he means The Magic Castle in Los Angeles, right?"

"That's the only one I know of," the man agreed.

"Well, I know for a fact that The Magic Castle didn't open until 1963, because I was one of the first magicians to perform there. So, either this note is a fake, or he's making plans for a lunch that couldn't happen for another six years at a place that didn't yet exist."

"Thanks, Harry," the man said. "I'll tell Duane he can keep his letter."

"I have an even better suggestion of what he could do with it," Harry said. "But I won't say it in front of these youngsters."

The man slogged his way across the room, clearly

crushed that his amazing find had turned out to be far less precious than advertised.

"Good work, kids," Harry said as he grabbed a cookie. He began to return to Max and Abe across the room but turned back. "And that's a nice tattoo, Cecilia," he said.

"Thanks," she said, her face brightening.

"I had no idea you were such a big fan of ... Walt Disney," he added with a chuckle as he walked away.

"Your uncle is a tough man to fool," Cecilia said.

"That's what I'm learning," I agreed.

"Want me to show you how to do that trick with the hypnotized knee?"

"Absolutely," I said as I followed her across the room.

If you had to pick a date and a time when I made the decision I wanted to be a magician, I think this was it.

CHAPTER FOUR

THE TELL-TALE PROP

IN LESS THAN TWO WEEKS, I had gone from knowing no one at the school to having two regular lunch mates. I'm not good at math, but I figured at this rate, I'd be pals with everyone in the school before the Christmas break.

Of course, that was unlikely.

In fact, while I did have two friends, I was about to make half as many enemies in a matter of minutes.

But I didn't know that at the time.

Nathan, Cecilia and I were seated at what had become our regular spot in the lunchroom. It wasn't a prime location, but we were in a corner, and it wasn't terribly loud, so it worked just fine.

Since our encounter in the principal's office, Nathan and I had discovered we shared two classes and that our lockers were within shouting distance of each other.

Cecilia and I shared one class—English—but the seating was alphabetical, so Marks sat far across the room from Hernandez. But we had the same lunch hour, as did Nathan. So, it only took a couple of days for the three of us to find our own table and work out a routine.

The routine was simple: Get through the lunch line (or run to your locker and get your bag lunch) as quickly as possible, grab our table and start talking about magic.

Nathan's early interest in how I did The French Drop had blossomed when Cecilia wowed him by bending a fork with her mind. Later I'd looked up that effect in one of Harry's hundreds of magic books. She had done a really good job with what was actually a pretty simple trick.

So now Nathan was also hooked on magic and that was just about all we discussed. Other topics—school-work, last night's TV shows, the World Series—popped up from time to time, but our real focus was on magic: Learning new tricks and trying to stump each other.

"I'm sort of full," Cecilia said as she pulled a

banana from her lunch bag. "You guys want to split this?"

"Sure," I said, and Nathan quickly agreed. He picked up the knife from his lunch tray, but Cecilia waved it away.

"No need," she said. "I'm learning how to cut through solid matter with my mind. I can't do thicker stuff yet, but I think I can mentally slice this banana pretty easily."

She set the banana on the table in front of her and concentrated on it, waving her hand over it twice. She paused for a second and then picked it up and proceeded to peel the banana. She turned it toward us.

With the peel out of the way, Nathan and I could clearly see the banana was neatly sliced into three segments, precisely where Cecilia had indicated with the wave of her hand.

"Slick," Nathan said as he grabbed his segment.

"Very nice," I agreed as I took my piece.

"I think it would have greater impact if it was cut into more pieces," Cecilia said as she took the remaining segment. "But not bad for a first try."

Before I could inquire about the specifics of the method, we were interrupted by a kid I didn't recognize. He was out of breath as he ran up to our table.

"Hey, Nathan," he said, not really paying attention

to me or Cecilia. "Simon smuggled in his radio and we're all listening to the World Series. It's in the last inning. We're in the courtyard if you want to join us."

And with that he was gone, scampering out of the door, and disappearing down the hall.

"Fantastic," Nathan said. He quickly finished off the rest of his lunch.

Nathan was far more interested in baseball than I was. He'd been complaining earlier that having to be in school was forcing him to miss the final game of the World Series. He had even considered pretending to be sick so he could stay home today.

"You two want to come?" Nathan said as he stood. "Final game. Could be historic."

I don't think either of us were wildly interested. But I often felt nervous being alone with Cecilia. So, I readily agreed.

"Sure thing," I said, perhaps overdoing my actual level of excitement.

"No sense breaking up the band," Cecilia agreed. She stood up and followed us out of the lunchroom.

THE COURTYARD WAS SIMPLY A SMALL PATIO space, neatly tucked between the older school building and the newer structure. This new building held the gym, the theater and the swimming pool.

It was a remarkably warm day for early November, with clear skies and no wind at all.

A small crowd of kids had gathered around one of the benches, some standing, some sitting on the ground.

On the bench sat a kid I recognized from my second day at school: Simon, the red-headed guy who I was pretty sure had been the one to sneak a look at Mrs. Sorenson's history essay questions.

Next to him on the bench was a beat-up boom box. On top of the boom box sat what looked like a big white handkerchief. And on top of that, a dirt-encrusted rock.

"It's the bottom of the ninth," came a professional voice from the boom box. "This is the last chance for the Diamondbacks, who are down two-to-one against the New York Yankees."

"They're doomed," said one of the kids.

"I don't think so," said Simon. "Diamondbacks are going to win it. I can feel it."

"No way," said the first kid.

"You wanna bet?" Simon replied.

"Sure, I'll take your money."

"Five bucks says the Diamondbacks pull it out and win the World Series."

"You're on," said the kid. "Five bucks says the Yankees win."

"Anyone else want to bet me?" Simon scanned the small crowd. There were murmurs of interest throughout the group. Several kids instantly agreed to the bet. If he lost, Simon was going to owe upwards of fifty dollars.

"I'll take that bet," Nathan said as he stepped forward.

Cecilia had reached out to stop him, but she was too late. She turned to me.

"Simon is a cheat," she said quietly. "Always has been."

"I know," I agreed. "I had an encounter with him right after I got here."

"It runs in the family," she said, still keeping her voice low. "Remember that fake letter to Dai Vernon at the magic meeting last week? That was Simon's father trying to sell it."

"Yikes," I said.

"Anyone else?" Simon asked, but he was interrupted by a roar from the boombox.

"There's a bunt by Miller, a throw to second," the

announcer yelled. "And now it's two on, with nobody out."

"Can you turn it up?" one of the kids asked as he reached for the boombox.

Simon slapped his hand away. "I'll do it," he said as he turned up the volume knob. "I just don't want anyone touching my Homer Hanky. It's an original, from the 1987 Twins playoffs. It's worth a lot of money."

He gently adjusted the white linen square, which was partially draped over the boombox. He also adjusted the rock, which appeared to be holding the handkerchief in place on this breezeless afternoon.

"It can't be worth that much," Cecilia said. "They produced over two million Homer Hankies."

"I don't know where you're getting your figures, Hernandez," Simon said with a sneer. "This is from the first printing, which was only one hundred. My dad got it for me."

Before she could reply, Simon held up his hand and turned back to the boombox.

"The score is now two-two," said the radio announcer. "Bottom of the ninth."

All the kids moved in closer, but Cecilia and I stood back.

"Something about this doesn't feel right," I said.

"I agree," Cecilia said. "I keep thinking about something your Uncle Harry said about how to use props in a magic show. That everything on stage must be there for a reason."

"And I keep thinking about one clever form of misdirection. I saw a mention of it in one of the magic books in my apartment. But I can't remember what it's called."

Her eyes went a little wide. "You have your own apartment?"

"It's a long story."

Before I could say more, the murmur started to get louder from the small crowd around us.

"Bases loaded," said the announcer. "A hit to center field. And that's it, folks, it's ending in a walk-off. The Diamondbacks have won this World Series, three to two over the New York Yankees!"

This produced a groan from the crowd as Simon reached over and spun the volume knob to zero. Which struck me as odd, as the On/Off switch was closer.

"That's it," Simon said with a wide grin. "Pay up, suckers."

All the kids who had taken Simon's bet began to dig into their pockets and their backpacks for money. Nathan pulled a five-dollar bill from his pocket and was just stepping forward to give it to Simon. But Cecilia reached out and grabbed him before he could hand over the money.

"Not so fast," she said. "Simon, this is a scam." She looked over at me. "Right, Eli?"

"I think so," I agreed. But I wasn't as positive as she was.

WHY IS CECILIA CONVINCED THAT SIMON IS PULLING A SCAM WITH THIS BASEBALL BET?

"A SCAM? OH YEAH?" SIMON SAID DEFIANTLY. "How do you figure?"

"The man I'm taking magic lessons from was telling me a principle of any good performance," Cecilia said. "And it's that every prop on the stage is there for a reason. And I couldn't figure out why that Homer Hanky is there on top of your boom box."

"It's my good luck charm," Simon said. He reached over and gave the piece of linen a fond tap. "It means a lot to me."

"Then why have you put a big dirty rock on top of it?"

"In case the wind tries to blow it away," Simon countered.

"But there is no wind," Cecilia shot back.

"It's called being prepared, Cecilia," Simon said. "You should try it some time."

"No," I interrupted. His last word—time—had triggered my memory. "It's called *time misdirection*. Which means making the audience think something is happening at one time, when in fact it's already happened. Like that baseball game."

I stepped toward the boom box. Simon reached

out to stop me. But Cecilia was already there, holding back his arm.

I picked up the rock and pulled back the Homer Hanky.

"Just as I thought," I said. "We weren't listening to this boom box's radio. We were listening to its cassette deck."

I gestured toward the top of the boom box. With the Homer Hanky gone, we could all see the push-button controls for the cassette tape deck. The PLAY button was depressed. I hit the STOP button and then pressed down on the REWIND button for several seconds.

Then I pressed down on the PLAY button, and a familiar voice came out of the speaker.

"A hit to center field. And that's it, folks, it's ending in a walk-off. The Diamondbacks have won this World Series, three to two over the New York Yankees!"

I hit the STOP button and turned to the group around me.

"Simon recorded the end of the game a few minutes ago. He then made us all believe we were listening to it live and for the first time," I explained.

"But he needed to cover up the cassette player part of the boom box," Cecilia added. "That's where the

Homer Hanky prop came in. And even though there's no wind today, Simon couldn't take any chance of the Homer Hanky coming off, exposing his scam. So, he put a filthy rock on top of his supposedly precious Homer Hanky."

"Save your money, everybody," I said.

They didn't need to hear this twice. All the kids quickly put their money away as Simon stood up and grabbed his boom box.

We watched him storm off.

"I doubt we've heard the last of Simon Hartwell," Cecilia said quietly. "Now, tell me how it is that a thirteen-year-old kid has his own apartment?"

"Only if you tell me how you psychically sliced that banana into three pieces," I countered.

But before either of us could answer, the bell rang, sending us off to our separate classes.

CHAPTER FIVE

THE GUY WHO CAME IN FROM THE COLD

"ELI, CAN YOU DO ME A FAVOR?"

I could hear my Aunt Alice's voice through the intercom next to my bed. But an instant before that, I heard her voice coming from the kitchen, one floor below.

The sound from the box had been a split second later, creating a weird sort of echo.

"Sure thing," I said loudly, not bothering to flip the switch on the intercom. If I could hear her one floor away, I figured she could hear me as well.

I shot down the steep stairs to the apartment she shared with Uncle Harry. She was already standing in the doorway. I could see pots bubbling on the stove behind her.

"Eli, be a dear and go over to Adrian's. Tell your

Uncle Harry that dinner will be ready in fifteen minutes."

I was oddly pleased by this request. This was the first "outside of the apartment" task she'd given me since my arrival a month before. Either she was starting to sense I could handle some responsibility. Or she just didn't feel like making the trek up and down those stairs herself.

It was probably a little of both.

"Sure thing," I said as I began to descend the stairs to ground level.

"Hang on," she added. "I'm feeling cold, so you better take a coat."

She reached around the doorframe to the hooks on the wall. She came back with my jacket in hand. I climbed back up the stairs, took it from her and then headed back down to the street.

She wasn't wrong. I felt a sharp nip in the air as I stepped out onto Chicago Avenue.

Although I was new to the neighborhood, I was finding that I liked living on a busy street.

To my right was The Parkway Theater, an actual movie theater right next to my new home. Incredible.

Next to that was Pepito's, a Mexican restaurant. We'd eaten there once since my arrival, and I hoped we'd go back soon. My Aunt Alice was an excellent cook, but I don't think Mexican food was something she'd ever attempt at home.

To my left, next to the magic store, was Adrian's, a neighborhood bar and grille which was a favorite of my Uncle Harry and his friends. Or his "cronies," as Aunt Alice called them. That was a word I had to look up. It's just another word for friends.

Beyond Adrian's there were several shops—a stamp collectors' store, a check cashing and mailing shop, a beauty parlor, a laundromat—with a drugstore on the corner. The drugstore had proven to be a good source for comic books and even carried issues of *Famous Monsters of Filmland* and *MAD Magazine*.

I immediately realized I really hadn't needed the jacket. It was just a few steps to Adrian's. I was inside before I had even gotten around to zipping up.

It took a second for my eyes to adjust to the dim light of the bar. But spotting Uncle Harry wasn't a problem. He and his friends—his cronies— always sat at the same table in the back.

There was no one else in the place, except for a waitress. She was behind the bar, reading a worn paper-back. I headed across the room to Harry.

"Ah, the Prodigal Nephew," Abe Ackerman said, looking up from the perpetual card game that absorbed the greater part of the Minneapolis Mystics' time.

That's what the group called themselves: The Minneapolis Mystics. It was basically just a bunch of old magicians who hung out in a bar, swapping stories and doing tricks. But I guess the name The Minneapolis Mystics made the whole thing sound more legitimate.

There were only three members in attendance this afternoon: The mind reader, Abe Ackerman. The card expert, Max Monarch. And my Uncle Harry, who I'd come to understand was sort of an all-around magician.

"I suspect your Aunt Alice has sent you over here to alert me to our impending dinner," Harry said as he set down his cards. "Your timing couldn't have been better. I've got nothing."

"I fold as well," Abe said. "Erdnase himself couldn't do anything with this hand. Once again, the dealer takes the pot. Seems a tad suspicious to me ..."

The others laughed at this as Max gathered up all the cards. He squared the deck as he looked over at me.

"Hey, Eli, want to see a card trick?"

I'd only had about a half dozen conversations with Max Monarch. I think every one of them had begun with "Hey, Eli, want to see a card trick?"

"Sure thing," I said. So far, Max and his tricks had never disappointed.

He spread the cards in front of me. "Take a card. Free choice."

Although I was new to this, I was beginning to suspect that—with a magician—there was rarely such a thing as a free choice. But I did my best to take the card that I wanted to take.

"Now look at it and memorize it."

I did as instructed, shielding the card from prying eyes. It was the Queen of Hearts.

"Now I need you to create a bond with that card," Max continued, as he casually mixed and remixed the deck of cards in his hands. "The simplest way to do that, I've found, is to name it. Have you got a name for it?"

I struggled to pull a name out of the air. I settled on the first one that came to me.

"Yes."

"Terrific. Remember the name and remember the card. And while you're doing all that remembering, place the card anywhere back in the deck."

He spread the cards in front of me. Just like before, I felt my choices weren't as free as they appeared. But I went ahead and slid the card into the spread, giving it an extra push to help bury it.

"Fantastic," Max said as he cut the cards. He then cut them again and squared the deck. "Now let's see how strong a bond you built with your card."

He picked up the card box from the table and slid the cards into it and closed the lid. Then he held up the box.

"Think about your card, Eli," he said, starting to sound a little dramatic. "Say the name in your head."

I did as instructed, repeating the name silently.

As I did that, I was surprised to see the top flap on the card box *pop* open, all by itself. A moment later, one card from the deck slowly began to rise up out of the box. It appeared to be moving on its own power.

"Keep thinking of the name," Max said.

I did as instructed. The card continued to rise up out of the box, finally revealing itself: It was the Queen of Hearts.

I couldn't help it—I actually gasped.

"Clearly you formed a strong connection with that card," Max said as he pulled it from the box. He handed it toward me. "So strong that I think you should keep it."

Before I could take the card, the door to the bar swung open and light flooded into the room.

It was a uniformed police officer. He scanned the room.

"Hey, you guys, has anyone come in here during the last thirty minutes or so?"

"Only this lad here, Officer Brophy," Abe said. "But I think we can vouch for him."

"No, the description I got was early thirties. About five-ten, sandy hair under a wool cap, in a worn green parka," Brophy said as he consulted his small notebook.

"What happened?" The waitress behind the bar had abandoned her paperback.

Brophy stepped further into the room, letting the door swing shut behind him.

"There was a robbery down the block a few minutes ago," he said.

"The drug store?" Harry asked.

The officer shook his head. "No, that check cashing place three doors down. You know, that hole in the wall. They wire money, do postage, have a mail drop, cash checks. Some guy came in, said he was just coming in to get out of the cold. Then the clerk says the guy pulled a gun on him. Cleaned him out. I'm stopping at all the nearby businesses to see if anyone has come in here since then."

"Nope. It's been quiet," the waitress said as she returned her attention to her book.

"Surely a place like that has a security system of some sort," Max said. "Cameras and such?"

Brophy crossed the room toward us.

"Usually, yes," he said. "But according to the clerk, the system is in the midst of being upgraded. So, nothing was operational."

"This clerk, he was alone in the shop?" Harry asked.

Brophy nodded. "The boss had to run some errands. So, he was all by himself in there. And tomorrow's payday for a lot of people, so they had more money than usual in the till. Nearly twelve thousand dollars, he says."

I wasn't following all this and turned to Harry.

"Some people don't have bank accounts," he explained quickly. "So, they use a shop like that one to cash their paychecks. The store takes a small percentage."

Harry turned back to Officer Brophy.

"So, our robber happened to show up on the same day that they had the most amount of cash in the till," Harry said. "And the least number of employees in the shop. And absolutely no operational security cameras."

"This robber was either very lucky. Or very knowledgeable," Max offered.

"True enough," Harry said. "In fact, the only person more knowledgeable was the clerk himself."

"So, you think he was working in cahoots with this robber?" Abe said.

"Possibly. Or perhaps there was no robber at all. Just a well-timed fiction on the part of the clerk."

"We considered that," Officer Brophy said. "The clerk has only worked there a couple months. But we searched the place: his locker, the other lockers, his backpack. Frisked him, even. The money was nowhere to be found. It's gone. Disappeared into thin air."

"Disappeared, along with the guy who came in from the cold," Abe said.

"Sure. If he even exists," Max said.

That's when it hit me. I looked over at Uncle Harry. His expression suggested he was having the same thought I was.

"Anyway, if you guys hear anything, just give me a holler," Officer Brophy continued. "But to be honest, given what we currently know, I don't think we'll ever arrest anyone for this crime."

"On the contrary," Harry said. "I think you can make an arrest right this minute." He looked over at me. "Do you agree, Eli?"

"I do," I said.

. . .

WHY ARE ELI AND HARRY SO CERTAIN THEY KNOW WHO ROBBED THE CHECK CASHING SHOP?

"IT'S THE CLERK," HARRY SAID DEFINITIVELY. "He's your robber."

"There was no one else," I added.

"I don't disagree," Brophy said. "But if it is, where's the money? There's no place to hide it. It's not a big shop."

"He mailed it," I said. "He mailed it to himself."

"I agree," Harry said. "In addition to cashing checks and wiring money, they sell postage in that shop. There's a mail pick-up in there. I've seen the mailman go in and out. And, because it's an official mail drop, that box is locked. Only the mailman can open it."

"So, all he had to do was take the money from the cash register and put it in an envelope," I said. "Then address it to himself, add postage and drop it into the mail slot."

"And a couple days later the US Postal Service conveniently delivers $12,000 in cash to his home address," Harry added.

Officer Brophy considered this idea for a long moment, then reached for his radio as he headed toward the door.

"Guys, I think we've got a lead on that robbery..."

We all watched him go. And then Max picked up

exactly where he'd left off before Brophy had come in from the cold.

"Here's your card, Eli," he said, handing me the Queen of Hearts. "Want me to teach you how to do the trick?"

"Absolutely," I said.

For the next few minutes, I had the good fortune of having one of the top card men in magic teach me a pretty basic—but still impressive—card trick. This was accompanied by remarks from both Abe and Harry, each offering fun flourishes and refinements.

We were so engrossed, I think we were all surprised when we looked up to see Aunt Alice staring down at us.

"This is what I get for not doing the job myself," she said. She was acting stern, but there was a smile in her eyes.

"We were just heading up," Harry lied.

"Oh, I'm sure you were," Aunt Alice said with a smirk.

Harry and I got up quickly.

"Thanks, Max," I said. "That's a great trick."

"It's a good trick. It'll only be great if you practice," Max said.

"I will," I promised.

As soon as we stepped outside, Aunt Alice insisted

I zip up my jacket, even though we were just steps away from home.

So, I complied. As I did, I glanced down the street, just in time to see Officer Brophy coming out of the check cashing store. He and another officer were escorting a young guy in handcuffs toward Brophy's patrol car.

"Looks like Brophy got his man," Harry said as we stepped into our building.

"Looks like it," I agreed.

"By the way, Eli, you never said. What name did you give your card?"

I was surprised by the question. "I don't know," I stammered. "I don't remember."

"Ah," Harry said, as he headed up the stairs. I followed, shutting the door behind me.

That wasn't really the truth. Of course I remembered the name I had given the Queen of Hearts.

I just hadn't admitted it.

It was Cecilia.

CHAPTER SIX

THE THIRTY-NINE DANCE STEPS

"ARE they going to give you a title in the program?"

Cecilia shook her head. "I don't know."

"Like 'Technical Advisor?'" I suggested. "'Magical Advisor?' 'Technical Magical Advisor?' 'Magical Technical Advisor,' maybe?"

"It hasn't come up yet."

We were snaking our way through the halls of Anthony Middle School, Cecilia in the lead, me struggling to keep up. We were headed toward the school's auditorium, where they were in the middle of rehearsals for the upcoming musical production of *"Oliver!"*

To be honest, I wasn't super interested in the show or the music. But when Cecilia told me she'd been asked to come up with a couple magic tricks for one segment, I was more than intrigued.

Moments later, I found myself standing next to her backstage, watching a rehearsal of the number she was working on.

In the scene, young Oliver Twist has met up with Mr. Fagin, who oversees a teen mob of expert thieves. During a song (*"You've Got To Pick a Pocket or Two"*), Fagin demonstrates the team's skill at picking his pocket. And at several points, Fagin also makes silk handkerchiefs appear—as if by magic—out of thin air.

At one point, he even twists a handkerchief so that one end is standing straight up in his fist. The end of the handkerchief then seems to take on a life of its own, moving and bending. It looked like it was struggling to get out of his hand. The actor playing Fagin pretended to pull a hair from one of the nearby kids and then mimed tying this invisible hair onto the tip of the disobedient handkerchief. Using the invisible hair like a leash, he was then able to control the handkerchief's movements, appearing to pull it first left and then right.

"That's a cool trick," I whispered.

"It's called The Dancing Hanky," Cecilia replied. "It's as old as the hills, but seemed like a good fit for this scene."

"Indeed," I agreed.

Finished with The Dancing Hanky, the actor—who I later learned was named Jake—continued dancing as he sang. He wore an ankle-length, dark green coat, which seemed to be tricked out with secret pockets from which he could make the handkerchiefs appear. Jake danced around the other kids, with the coat sailing around him, high enough off the floor that I could clearly see his fancy footwork.

"Good, good," Cecilia said quietly as Jake made two more handkerchiefs appear at the tips of his fingers.

"Let's stop for a second," came a voice from the audience. "Is Cecilia here?"

"I am," Cecilia said as she stepped forward.

I peered around the curtain as a teacher I recognized climbed up the steps to the stage.

"Cecilia," she said. "We've got a short musical section here with no lyrics. I'm wondering if there's anything in your bag of tricks that Jake could use to fill it? It's about forty beats long."

"No problem, Mrs. Katz," Cecilia said quickly. She seemed confident that a solution to the problem was within easy reach. She walked around Jake for a few seconds, and then an idea struck her.

"Why don't we use a couple of the handkerchiefs

for a quick magic trick, where Fagin appears to use the handkerchiefs to cut Oliver in half?"

"Sounds gruesome. And also lovely," Mrs. Katz said.

Cecilia turned to me. I was still standing in the wings. "It's something I read in a Jim Steinmeyer book," she explained.

I didn't know who she meant, but I nodded anyway.

"Can you demonstrate it for us?" Mrs. Katz asked.

Cecilia proceeded to do just that.

Stepping into the role of Fagin, she took two long, colorful handkerchiefs and tied them together. She wrapped the handkerchiefs around Oliver Twist's midsection. Then—with a quick move—she appeared to pull the handkerchiefs right through his body.

This produced spontaneous applause from the assembled cast. Mrs. Katz smiled and nodded. "That's terrific. And just about one beat short of what we need."

"I can make up the difference," Jake said. He turned to Cecilia. "Now show me how you did that."

I watched from the sidelines for the next few minutes as Cecilia demonstrated the steps in the illusion. Jake picked up the moves with ease. He was a natural performer.

They ran the piece again, this time with piano accompaniment, and it looked terrific. Jake danced around as he performed the trick, his coat twirling around his ankles in time with the music.

"He's very good," I whispered.

Cecilia nodded. "He's the best actor in the school. Your uncle Harry once told me, it's easier to make a good actor into a magician than it is to turn a magician into a good actor."

Before I could fully process that idea, the teacher stepped back onto the stage.

"Fantastic," Mrs. Katz said. She was beaming. "We're just one beat short—we're at thirty-nine steps and it should be forty."

"I'll work on that tonight," Jake said.

"Thanks Jake." She turned to the whole cast. "And thanks everyone. Great rehearsal. Our first full-dress rehearsal is tomorrow. And don't forget: run your lines!"

And with that the large cast began to disperse.

As they did, for the first time I noticed Simon Hartwell.

He was easy to spot with his bright red hair.

He was standing across the large stage, in the other wing, directly across from me. Simon was glaring in my direction, but it wasn't clear if I was the subject of his intense stare or not.

And then he was gone.

I spun around and followed Cecilia, who was still chatting with Jake. We turned two corners, which deposited us into a small, curtained cubicle backstage. It contained a chair, a make-up mirror, a light, and a coat rack.

Jake took off his green coat and hung it up next to a black suit. He took off his hat and his wig and hung the hat next to the coat. On the table was a fake beard, among other make-up items.

"You've got your own dressing room?" Cecilia said as she looked around. "Snazzy."

"It doesn't really count as a room, but it's close to the stage, so they gave it to me," Jake said. "I'm the only one who has to make a quick change."

"In addition to playing Fagin, Jake also plays the owner of the funeral parlor, Mr. Sowerberry," Cecilia explained. I think she realized that Jake had no idea who I was. "Jake, this is Eli. He and I do magic together."

"Nice to meet you, Eli," Jake said. He grabbed his backpack, which had been shoved under the table. "Cecilia, do you have time to go over that new bit? I've got the basics, but it would help to run it a couple more times in front of someone who knows what I'm doing right. And what I'm doing wrong."

"No problem. Let's go where there's a bit more light," she said.

SUNLIGHT POURED INTO THE HALLWAY RIGHT outside the auditorium. Classes had let out more than an hour before, so there was plenty of room for Jake to practice the routine. And for Cecilia to offer him notes.

Since I was the only other person there, I got to play the part of Oliver Twist, being cut in half by Mr. Fagin. We tried it a couple times, with Cecilia counting beats as Jake went through the moves.

And each time it was one beat short.

"I don't know what I'm doing differently," Jake said as he re-set the trick. "I nearly got it to forty the first time and can't seem to get back there."

"We'll figure it out," Cecilia said. "It's like a dance. We just need to figure out each step."

Jake began the trick one more time.

"Well, that makes perfect sense," said a voice down the hall. "It's type casting: Have the orphan play an orphan."

We all turned to see that Simon Hartwell was watching us from a short distance away.

It took me a moment to realize when he said 'orphan,' he was talking about me. I may be wrong, but I think that was the first time I'd heard that word said aloud since my parents died.

It felt odd.

"Take a hike," Cecilia said, immediately coming to my defense. "You're just jealous because Jake got cast in two roles and you didn't even pass the audition to get one. You're not even in the chorus. Just stuck in the backstage crew where you won't scare the audience."

"Buzz off, Hartwell," Jake added as he completed the illusion, appearing to pull the handkerchiefs right through me.

"Who's going to make me?" Simon Hartwell said with a sneer. He was acting pretty tough for someone who wasn't surrounded by his friends.

"I'm happy to do it," Jake said. He tossed the handkerchiefs on the ground and marched directly up to Simon.

They stared at each other for a long moment. Jake was easily a couple inches taller than Simon. And both were bigger than me.

Simon finally backed down.

"I'll leave you to your little dance with your pretty

handkerchiefs," Simon said as he turned and walked away.

"And I'll be sure to wave to you when I'm on stage taking my bows, while you're hidden away in the dark backstage," Jake added with a laugh.

He watched Simon go and then came back and picked up the handkerchiefs.

"What a bully," Cecilia said.

"As my dad always says, 'Bullies are mostly bull,'" Jake said. "Let's try that trick one more time."

I smiled. Despite yet another run-in with Simon Hartwell, I was having a good afternoon. Not only had I gained a new friend, but I was also learning the inner workings of a pretty cool magic trick.

CECILIA HAD A SPARE TICKET FOR OPENING Night, and she invited me as her guest. This nighttime adventure required some negotiations with Aunt Alice and Uncle Harry, as it was the first time I would be venturing out on my own after dark.

The solution we agreed on was that Aunt Alice would drive me there and pick me up after the show. I recognized this was a truly dorky option. But it was the only one available, so I jumped on it.

It was also the first snowfall of the season, a new experience for me. There was about two inches of the white, fluffy stuff lining the streets and sidewalks. It might have slowed Aunt Alice's driving time, but not by much. As a long-time resident of Minnesota, she never let snow intimidate her.

We pulled up to the school and she handed me her cell phone as I stepped out of the car.

"Call Harry's phone when it's over. One of us will come and get you."

"Sure thing," I said as I quickly stepped away from the car. Although I was virtually unknown at the school, I still didn't want anyone to see me being dropped off by someone who could easily be mistaken for my grandmother.

I made my way to the auditorium, keeping an eye out for Cecilia. As it turned out, she spotted me before I spotted her. She was dressed up a bit for the occasion, but still sported her bright red high-top sneakers.

Jake was standing next to her. I was surprised that he wasn't in costume yet. He was looking pretty pale. I thought it might be stage fright.

"There's a problem," Cecilia said, sounding a little out of breath. "I think the play might be canceled."

"What happened?"

As if to answer me, the door to the auditorium

swung open. Out marched Principal Moore and Mrs. Katz. He saw us standing there and pointed in our direction.

"You. Follow me," he said firmly as he continued down the hall.

I was pretty sure he had pointed only at Jake, but the three of us followed the teacher and the principal down the hall in silence.

The long corridor was only partially lit and there was no light coming from any of the classrooms we passed. However, the lights were on in the main office. We followed the two adults in, the door swinging shut behind us with a solid snick.

Principal Moore stepped behind the main counter and swung a monitor around. He looked at us for the first time. I think he was a little surprised to see that all three of us had followed them into the office.

"Jake, someone took the air out of Mrs. Katz's car tires," Principal Moore said sharply. "We've looked at the surveillance video of the back parking lot. Can you explain this?"

He tapped a key on the keyboard and a video image appeared on the monitor. It was a high-angle, grainy black and white shot of the school's back parking lot.

Nothing happened for several seconds, and then a

figure appeared, walking away from the school and into the parking lot. Even from the high angle, it was clearly Fagin: The hat, the beard, the wig. Even the long coat, dragging in the snow behind the steadily moving figure.

The figure looked around and then squatted down next to a car, obviously fiddling with one of the tires.

Jake studied the image closely.

"Does that look like anyone you know?" Principal Moore said.

"It's you. In your Fagin costume," Mrs. Katz said. "I'm very disappointed in you, Jake."

"I didn't do this," Jake said, his voice faltering.

"The video says you did," Principal Moore replied.

"I don't know how to prove it's not me," Jake said, starting to really sound distressed. "Maybe by the footprints?"

"No," Cecilia said with a sad shake of her head. "The coat wiped them away as you walked. I mean, as whoever it was walked."

"Actually," I said suddenly. I was surprised at myself for speaking up. "If anything, the video proves that it absolutely <u>wasn't</u> Jake."

• • •

WHY IS ELI CERTAIN THAT IT ISN'T JAKE IN THE VIDEO?

"How do you figure?" Principal Moore said.

"Whoever is wearing that coat is clearly shorter than Jake," I said, pointing at the screen. The figure was heading back to the school. With the hat and the wig and the beard, it was impossible to see his face. But one thing was obvious.

"See how the hem of the coat is dragging on the ground?" I continued. "When I saw Jake rehearsing the other day, I could clearly see his feet and ankles when he danced in that coat. Whoever that person is, he's easily a couple inches shorter than Jake."

"And that costume is hanging backstage, right out in the open," Cecilia offered. "Anyone with access to the backstage area could have grabbed it."

"Too bad the footprints in the snow are erased by the dragging of the coat," Jake said.

"That's true," Cecilia agreed. "But he did squat down four times, once by each of the tires. The coat wouldn't have erased <u>those</u> footprints."

"Is there anyone you can think of who might have wanted to frame you?" Principal Moore said.

"I can think of one guy," Jake said. "I had a run-in with Simon Hartwell the other day."

Mrs. Katz nodded at this suggestion. "And I suspected Simon was angry with me for not casting him in the show," she said. She then lowered her voice. "But to be honest, he really wasn't very good."

"Well, I'm going to track down Mr. Hartwell and take a serious look at his shoes," the principal said as he returned the monitor to its proper position. "Don't you have a show to do?"

All eyes turned to the large clock on the wall.

"Oh, my, it's almost curtain time," Mrs. Katz exclaimed. "We've got to get the show started!"

This was followed by a mad race down the hall, toward the auditorium.

Here's my mini review: The show was terrific. And it didn't seem to suffer from the loss of Simon Hartwell on the backstage crew one bit.

Jake was Outstanding in both roles (the dour funeral director, Mr. Sowerberry, and the antic Fagin). But throughout the show—right through the thunderous standing ovation the cast received—I couldn't shake one persistent thought.

For the first time ever, I began to think I might like to appear—in some form—up on a stage like that.

I was beginning to understand I really wanted to be in front of an audience.

CHAPTER SEVEN

THE THIN MINT MAN

"SORRY ABOUT THE POTHOLES."

"I don't think the potholes are the problem. I think it's me," I said, as the coin slipped off the back of my hand for maybe the millionth time.

I was seated in the passenger seat, with Aunt Alice driving. It was spring in Minnesota. And there were potholes. Lots and lots of potholes. Which made our journey to the grocery store a bumpy ride indeed.

I was attempting to master a new move Uncle Harry had taught me: rolling a coin across the back of my fingers.

When he did it, it looked amazing. It was as if the coin (he used a fifty-cent piece) was dancing across the back of his hand.

When I attempted the moves (with a quarter, which better fit my hand), it looked nothing like that. It looked more like a coin on its last legs, sputtering and staggering across my fingers, clearly in pain.

We hit another pothole, which sent the quarter sailing out of my hand and onto the floor of the car, well out of sight.

"We're almost there," Aunt Alice said. "We can find it when we park."

She was right. After she found a parking spot, I was able to find the quarter. Although it took me bending like a pretzel and craning my neck to find the scuffed coin. It had wedged itself far under the car's front seat.

Once retrieved, I followed her across the parking lot toward the front of the grocery store, which had as its mascot (for some odd reason) a bright red owl.

I was tasked with pushing the cart while Aunt Alice bounced from one side of the aisle to the other, consulting her list and comparing prices. She would sometimes stand for several seconds, doing math in her head as she weighed the cost and size of one product against its larger counterpart.

I was glad she wasn't asking me for help. I'm not what you'd call a math whiz.

While she studied the products, I spent those few

free moments returning to my work with the quarter. Again and again, I attempted to make it roll—smoothly—across my knuckles.

It wasn't going well.

"This is much harder than it looks," I remember saying to Uncle Harry the first time I attempted it.

"I think that's the point," he replied. "A quick display of mastery is an excellent way to get an audience on your side right from the start. If you look like a pro, they assume you must be proficient. In something. And with any luck that will be magic. Although I've seen many a magician who failed badly in that regard."

I looked up to see that Aunt Alice had made her way further down the aisle. So I put the quarter back into my fist and followed behind her with the cart.

This pattern was repeated throughout our shopping expedition: Aunt Alice would stop long enough for me to get about twenty seconds of practicing in. And then we'd be off to find the next item on her list.

Finally, we reached the checkout line, which was long. I figured I might get a minute or two of solid practice while we waited. But that was not to be.

"Oh, look," Aunt Alice said. She pointed to an area on the other side of the checkout aisles. "Girl Scout cookies. Is it that time of year already?"

She immediately began to dig into her purse, finally handing me a crumpled five-dollar bill.

"Your Uncle Harry loves Tagalongs. Be a dear and go get a box for him."

I sighed and returned my quarter—still warm from all the practice—back into my pocket as I squeezed past her.

Two Girl Scouts had set up a folding table near the exit. A large, slightly askew banner hung behind them. The table was stacked high with cookie boxes. Several cartons were piled behind the table. Two women— maybe they were scout leaders—stood behind the girls and in front of the banner.

I recognized one of the girls from my algebra class, which made me panic immediately. I had no idea what I should say to her. However, I knew I needed to buy a box of cookies. I calmed a bit, realizing that would provide a good conversation starter.

The problem was, I couldn't remember the name of the cookies Aunt Alice had asked me to buy. It had been less than thirty seconds ago, but the name— whatever it was—had flown out of my mind.

There was a man in front of me just starting his order, so I was able to peer around him to read the names of the cookies on the boxes. I hoped one would jog my memory.

"A box of Thin Mints," the man said.

The girls, who were both a little giggly, had clearly established a division of labor. One of them retrieved the requested box of cookies. The other took the money and made change.

The two women—perhaps they weren't scout leaders, but maybe just mothers—chatted back and forth. They only occasionally glanced over at the transaction.

The man gave the money girl a ten-dollar bill, while the cookie girl handed him a box of cookies. They were Thin Mints. That wasn't what Aunt Alice had told me to buy. I continued to scan the names on the stacks of boxes on the table.

"Here's your change," the money girl said. "Seven dollars."

"Oh, are you getting short on one-dollar bills?" the man asked. "I have some extras."

"That would be great," the money girl said.

I shifted my weight to my other foot, peering around on the other side of the Thin Mint Man. I saw a stack of Samoas and Trefoils. Those cookie names didn't ring any bells.

"Here's ten ones and I'll take back the ten I gave you," the man said.

I could see two more stacks of boxes: Do-Si Dos

and All Abouts. Those were weird names for cookies, I thought. And also not the ones Aunt Alice asked me to get.

"Oh, wait, sir," the money girl said. "You only gave me nine ones."

Something clicked in my head. I stopped looking at cookie boxes and started to pay attention to the transaction going on in front of me.

"Did I? Sorry about that," he said, sounding very apologetic. He counted out another one-dollar bill and handed it to her. "Here you go. In fact, I'll give you that and I'll give you the ten you gave me. That makes twenty. And then I'll just take a twenty from you."

The money girl did what he suggested, taking the bills he offered. She then pulled a twenty-dollar bill from the cigar box they used as a till.

Before she could hand it to him, I surprised myself by suddenly speaking up.

"Don't give him the twenty. He's pulling a fast one on you."

WHY IS ELI CONVINCED THE THIN MINT MAN IS DOING SOMETHING DISHONEST?

My exclamation immediately got the attention of the mothers, who stopped chatting and turned my way. It also sparked the interest of the store manager, who had just been passing by.

"What's going on here?" he asked.

"I think he is trying to cheat them out of seven dollars," I said quickly. "And a box of cookies."

"I did no such thing," the Thin Mint Man said. "I was helping them out by giving them some ones."

"Maybe," I said. "But you then blurred the lines between the two transactions. And I think you did it on purpose."

"Explain to me what he did," the store manager said.

I took a deep breath and then reconstructed the transaction as best I could.

"He bought a box of cookies for three dollars," I began.

"Thin Mints," added the money girl.

"He gave her a ten-dollar bill and she gave him seven ones as change."

"Seems fair so far," the store manager said.

"That's because it was fair up to that point," I

agreed. "And then he asked if they needed any one-dollar bills. They said yes. And he gave them back the seven ones, plus three more ones he had. Making ten dollars."

"And I gave him the ten-dollar bill in exchange for the ones," the money girl said. "But then I counted them, and there were only nine dollars."

"A simple mistake on my part," the Thin Mint Man said. "I immediately made up the difference."

"He did," I agreed. "But this is where he blurred the two transactions. He gave her the missing ones <u>and</u> the ten-dollar bill and asked for the twenty. But if you add it up, that doesn't work."

"How do you mean?" the Store Manager said.

"If he takes the twenty, the Girl Scouts are now short seven dollars. He's made seven dollars on the transaction."

The store manager considered this for a long moment. "So, when he added the ten to the three ones, he was essentially giving them thirteen dollars in exchange for twenty dollars?"

"Making seven dollars in the process," I added.

The Store Manager turned to the Thin Mint Man. "I think you need to give back the cookies. And the money. Then get out of here. And don't come back."

The Thin Mint Man grumbled, but he didn't put

up a fight. The Store Manager stuck around to make sure the process was fair. And then we all watched as the Thin Mint Man scurried out of the store.

A few moments later I found Aunt Alice, who was just finishing bagging her groceries. I added two boxes of cookies to the bulging bags and handed her two dollars in change.

"Oh, you got the Tagalongs, thank you," Aunt Alice said. She looked at the change and then at the two boxes of cookies. "And did you buy another box with your own money?"

I shook my head. "One of the Girl Scouts is in my algebra class. She gave me a free box of Thin Mints."

"Oh, do you think she likes you?"

I shrugged. "Hard to tell. But she did say she likes the way I do math."

I could tell this answer didn't really compute with Aunt Alice.

"Well, that's nice, dear. Give me a hand with these bags, please."

I helped her lug the groceries out to the car and then pulled the quarter out of my pocket. It would be a ten-minute ride home. So that gave me ten minutes of uninterrupted practice rolling a coin across the back of my hand.

I knew the potholes would make the challenge even harder. But I figured if I could make the trick work with the spring potholes in Minneapolis, I could make it work anywhere.

CHAPTER EIGHT

THE HOUND OF THE MORRISONS

"YOU KNOW, I was a magician's assistant when I first met Eli's Uncle Harry," Aunt Alice said.

She glanced into the rear-view mirror, to make sure Nathan understood she was talking to him.

"I did not know that," Nathan replied quietly from the back seat of the car.

I was sitting next to my aunt, who was kindly chauffeuring us to what was—sort of—our first magical gig. She had been attempting, mostly unsuccessfully, to get more than a single sentence out of Nathan the entire trip.

"Cecilia is a very lucky magician indeed to have two fine assistants," Aunt Alice continued. This was said with more of a smile than I felt was needed. "Have you each been assigned key duties?"

"We're just helping her to unpack and repack all her stuff," I said. "It's not a paid position."

"Plus, she needs us to keep the kids away from her props while she does balloon animals," Nathan added.

"Important tasks indeed," Aunt Alice replied. But I could tell her concentration had returned to her driving. She slowed as she looked at house numbers.

"I believe this is the one," she said, gesturing to a large, modern-looking house. There were no steps, just a long driveway which led up to the garage and the house to which it was attached.

"The spring rains have done a number on their lawn," Aunt Alice said as she brought the car to a stop. "It looks like a mudslide, waiting to happen."

"Yes, the party was supposed to be in the backyard, but it's all too muddy" I said. "So, they've moved it into the basement Rec Room instead."

"A wise move," Aunt Alice agreed. "Outdoor shows can be a headache, even under the best of conditions." She glanced at her watch. "I will be back to pick you up at four. Call if you need me to come earlier."

I nodded as I got out of the car. Nathan had already scrambled out of the backseat and was waiting for me on the sidewalk.

"And stick to the driveway," Aunt Alice added.

"You don't want to drag mud into Mrs. Morrison's house."

And with that last piece of advice offered, she drove away.

A FEW MOMENTS LATER, NATHAN AND I FOUND ourselves standing at the front door. We looked at each other, not quite sure what to do. And then I took the leap and rang the doorbell.

I could hear the buzz of the bell far behind the door. This was followed instantly by the sound of barking.

Then the door swung open, and Mrs. Morrison looked down at us. She appeared somewhat frazzled. In the distance, I could hear little kids, laughing and screaming. Shrieking, actually. If she had been listening to that for the last hour, I could see why she looked stressed. And the barking of the dog didn't seem to be helping.

"Miles, be quiet," she snapped. She then turned to us and switched to a smile. "You must be Cecilia's assistants."

"That's us," I said.

"She just got here," Mrs. Morrison said. "I told her

the kids will be done eating in about ten minutes. She's in the basement, setting up."

She gestured for us to enter, at the same time pointing to the stairs which led to the house's lower level.

We got halfway to the stairs when the source of the barking raced toward us. The dog—I'm guessing it was Miles— ran straight for me. He jumped up, planting his paws right on my stomach and nearly knocking me over. He was brown and tan and furry and super friendly.

The dog grinned up at me. I gave him a tentative pet on the head. This made him lean into me even more.

"Patrick, will you come here and take Miles?! Let's put him in the garage for the duration of the party," Mrs. Morrison said. She looked around. "Patrick, can you take care of Miles? Please."

A teenage kid appeared from upstairs, followed by what I'm guessing were his friends. They were older than me, probably in high school.

One of the teens—I'm guessing this was Patrick— lazily stepped forward. He and his friends were all dressed similarly, in light-colored khakis and t-shirts. Patrick sported what appeared to be the latest and most expensive sneakers. They were white and looked new.

"What?" he whined.

"Put Miles in the garage for the duration," she repeated. She then turned as she shooed the dog off me. "Not to worry, he has a bed out there. And food and water. He even has his own little doggie door, so he can go in and out whenever he likes."

I wasn't sure why she was offering this information, but I nodded agreeably. Perhaps she was concerned I thought she might be mistreating the dog in some way.

Nathan and I headed down the stairs. As we did, I could still hear Mrs. Morrison giving instructions to the teenagers.

"And Patrick, you and your friends stay away from the food on the patio. That's for the kids. And I'm saving some for your father."

Her voice became distant as we ventured down and down, into the basement.

"Do we need to set up chairs or anything?" I asked.

Cecilia shook her head. "No chairs. Harry said to make sure the kids sit on the floor."

"Why is that?" Nathan asked.

"In case any of them try to run up here while I'm doing a trick," Cecilia explained. "Harry said sitting in chairs makes it too easy to get up. You gain a couple of seconds to react if they have to get up from a position on the floor."

That made sense to me.

We helped her to unpack the two crates she had brought, setting out the tricks on a table next to what was going to be her stage area. Cecilia arranged the tricks in show order, occasionally consulting a hand-written list. She stared at the tricks for a long moment, and then quickly re-arranged the order of two of them.

Before I could ask the reason for the change, we heard some shrieks from upstairs and moments later a flock of small kids raced down the stairs and into the large Rec Room.

And—just like that—the show was off and running.

Cecilia did a fantastic job, balancing fun magic tricks while keeping control of the rowdy six- and seven-year-olds. Nathan and I watched from the side-lines as Cecilia went through trick after trick.

She opened with Hippity Hop Rabbits, which I

had seen Uncle Harry demonstrate in his magic shop. Cecilia had the kids screaming with delight as the images of a black bunny and a white bunny magically swapped places.

The kids yelled out their thoughts on how the trick was being done. However, the trick was designed to refute their ideas at every turn, which delighted the kids even more. It was really adorable.

Less adorable were the comments made by Patrick and his teenage buddies. They had crept downstairs and scowled at the show from their impromptu seats on the steps. They were clearly too cool to be impressed by anything as juvenile as a kid's magic show.

Cecilia then wowed the kids with a magic coloring book. The oversized book first appeared to be filled with blank pages. Then she flipped through it again and it was now filled with line drawings. And then she flipped through it one last time, to demonstrate that all the drawings were now completely colored in.

As with the previous trick, this produced screams of delight from the kids ... and a steady stream of unnecessary (and occasionally unkind) remarks from the teenagers.

I was considering what I might say if I went over

and told them to knock it off. But Mrs. Morrison beat me to it.

"You boys go upstairs and find something else to do," she said in a loud whisper. "And stay away from the food on the patio," she added as they grumbled their way up the stairs.

Cecilia then did an amazing trick with a balloon: She appeared to push a long, thin needle completely through the inflated balloon, without the balloon popping. She spun the balloon around on the stick, so they could see the needle went all the way through and came out on the other side. She inserted two more needles through the balloon, again without any explosion.

Finally, Cecilia popped the balloon, showering the kids in the front row with confetti.

She had this tiny audience in the palm of her hand.

"She's very good at this," Nathan whispered to me.

"Yes. Yes, she is," I agreed.

"I think that's the one for me," he added quietly.

"What do you mean?" I turned and looked at him, trying to read his expression. As it usually was with Nathan, that was impossible.

"Kids magic," Nathan finally said. "It feels right somehow."

"Ah," I said.

Mrs. Morrison headed up the stairs and returned several moments later, bearing a large birthday cake. She nodded at Cecilia, who seamlessly wrapped up a nesting boxes trick.

"Now we're going to have a little contest," Cecilia said. "We're going to sing Happy Birthday, and I want you to show me who can sing the *quietest*."

She led them in the song. The tamed kids whispered the song along with her, each one trying to make the least amount of sound possible.

"Fantastic," Cecilia said at the conclusion of the song. "Now it's time for cake! And then come back and I'll make each one of you your very own balloon animal."

This produced cheers from the kids as they ran across the room to where Mrs. Morrison had set up the cake.

This was our cue to quickly move in and pack up all of Cecilia's props. As we did, she got ready for a long session of blowing up balloon animals.

"Great show," I said as I carefully placed the magic props into the carrying case.

Cecilia shrugged. "I don't know. It was better than the last one, which is all I'm striving for."

"You really had them under your control the whole time," Nathan added.

"With kids shows, I think that's the greatest trick of all," Cecilia said.

We got the props packed up just in time. Moments later, the kids started streaming back from the cake table. Each one was bubbling with their own request for a custom balloon animal.

Nathan and I lugged the two cases up the stairs, setting them by the front door. We were going to head back down, but the sound of a very angry Mrs. Morrison stopped us in our tracks.

"Who ate those last three pieces of pizza?" she bellowed as she moved through the house. She looked right through us and turned her attention to the stairway which led up to the second floor. "Patrick, did you and your friends eat those last pieces of pizza?" she yelled. "I told you I was saving them for your father. Patrick?!"

I couldn't help but look up the stairs to see what his response might be. His bright white sneakers appeared first as he ambled down the stairs.

"We didn't touch them," he whined.

"Well, someone took them."

There was a short pause and then Patrick tilted his head toward the door to the garage. "It was Miles."

"The dog?" Mrs. Morrison said incredulously.

"He must have gotten out through his dog door,"

Patrick said. "I was upstairs, and I spotted him out on the patio. He swiped the pieces of pizza from the table. I came down to scold him. But he ran around the side of the house, across the front lawn and back through his dog door into the garage. I followed him and when I got to the garage, he jumped up on me. I could smell the garlic on his breath," he added.

"He's a bad dog," Mrs. Morrison muttered. "Well, there will be no dinner for him tonight, that's for sure."

Nathan turned to me, gesturing that I should say something. We couldn't let that innocent dog be punished.

"The dog didn't do it," I blurted out. "In fact, I'd be willing to bet he never even left the garage. He's innocent."

WHY IS ELI CONVINCED THAT THE DOG DIDN'T STEAL THE PIECES OF PIZZA FROM THE PATIO?

"How in the world would you know that?" Mrs. Morrison said. "You were downstairs the entire time."

"That's true," I said. "But I know that your back-yard, your side yard, and the front are really muddy. If Miles had run through there, his paws would have been filthy. Then, if Miles had jumped up on your son —like he claims—there would be muddy paw prints on his khakis. Which there aren't."

"Maybe I mis-spoke," Patrick said quickly. "Miles tried to jump up on me, but I pushed him away before he could get me all dirty."

"Perhaps. But did you also go out and buy an identical pair of sneakers in the last hour? Because if you followed the dog from the backyard to the garage, your shoes would be muddy as well. And they're clearly not."

Mrs. Morrison looked from her son to me, then glanced down at his bright white sneakers.

"Go upstairs," she said flatly. "We'll discuss this later."

It looked like Patrick had a snappy reply ready, but he decided against it. He turned and disappeared up the stairs. The last thing we saw of him were his clean, white shoes.

"So, I guess you guys are more than magicians," Mrs. Morrison said, clearly trying to make light of the situation. "You're also detectives."

"We're not magicians," Nathan corrected. "We're magicians' assistants."

"Call us Magicians in Training," I suggested. "And we're missing our session on balloon animals right now."

Nathan and I headed down the stairs and spent the next half hour watching Cecilia create animal after animal out of balloons.

"How was the show?" Aunt Alice asked as we climbed back into her car.

"I think I have decided that I want to be a kid's magician," Nathan announced. He sounded more upbeat than normal.

"How about you, Eli? Did you learn anything?"

I thought back to the show Cecilia had just put on. Thirty minutes of great tricks, all while managing twenty squirmy, noisy little kids. And then an hour of balloon animals.

"I think I'm beginning to realize that being a magician can be a tough job," I said.

Aunt Alice glanced over while she was driving and then patted my hand warmly.

"You'll have to tell Harry," she said quietly.

"Why is that?"

"Because I know he'll agree."

CHAPTER NINE

THE BIG SLEEPOVER

"THIS IS A LITTLE OVERWHELMING," Nathan said quietly.

"I second that emotion," I agreed.

This was a day of firsts for both of us.

We were at our first magic convention.

We were literally surrounded by the largest group of magicians we'd ever seen.

And we were standing in our first Dealers Room.

The Dealers Room was filled with magic dealers from all over. They each had a booth where they demonstrated and sold their tricks, their illusions, and their other products which would be of interest to magicians.

The place was swarming with excited magicians,

looking for the latest and greatest tricks. It was loud. It was hot.

It was amazing.

As Nathan had observed, it was all pretty overwhelming.

The convention—The Wizards' Weekend—was taking place in Minneapolis, just miles from home. However, because Uncle Harry was one of the people in charge of the event, he was staying at the convention hotel for the whole weekend.

And I got to stay with him. And experience my first Wizards' Weekend.

Or as my Aunt Alice called it, The Big Sleepover.

"Why do you call it that?" I had asked the first time she said it.

"Because it's essentially like a teenage sleepover: Everyone stays up all night, eating bad food and playing games. And no one ever gets any sleep."

It was still the first day of the convention, so I wasn't sure about the sleep thing. But in the few hours we'd been there, I'd seen loads of junk food.

And plenty of playing cards.

Lots and lots of playing cards.

The convention seemed to have three key areas: The Dealers Room, where magic was bought and sold.

The Ballroom, where magicians performed and gave lectures. And the lobby.

The lobby was where magicians gathered to show tricks to each other.

Harry said this practice was called *sessioning*.

There were *a lot* of magicians, seated around numerous tables in the lobby, sessioning like crazy.

And they were demonstrating *a lot* of mostly card tricks. They had been doing it since we'd arrived. And, according to Uncle Harry, it would continue all through the night ... and all through the weekend. Without stop.

Trick after trick after trick. Each magician trying to top the others.

There was one card trick in particular I wanted to talk to Uncle Harry about. I was impressed with the trick. But I was more impressed with the fact that it had been performed by an eight-year-old kid.

He was really good. Even though it had happened two hours ago, the trick was still buzzing around in my brain.

However, although Nathan and I were standing right next to Uncle Harry in the Dealers Room, it didn't look like I'd be talking to him about that card trick any time soon.

That's because it turned out that my Uncle Harry was famous. He was a star. At least, in the magic world.

Out on the street, most people probably wouldn't give him a second look.

But here at a magic convention, he couldn't walk two feet without someone stopping him to say hello. Or wanting to shake his hand. Or to ask him some magic-related question.

We'd been in the Dealers Room for almost thirty minutes with Harry. And in that whole time, we'd moved about six feet.

I'd never stood next to a celebrity before. And here's something I quickly learned: When you stand next to someone famous, you become almost invisible.

I wanted to venture further into the room and explore all the magic. And I got the sense that Nathan wanted to do the same.

I was about to tug at Harry's sleeve to get permission to head off on our own. He was listening to yet another person who wanted to tell him how they had gotten into magic after seeing him on something called *The Ed Sullivan Show.*

Before I could get his attention, he suddenly looked down at the two of us.

"Let's get out of here, boys," he said. "I've had

enough adulation for one day. Eli, keep talking to me, so I can ignore people as we make our escape."

He continued to look at me as we headed toward the door. Although people noticed him, they left him alone, because he appeared to be in deep conversation with a young kid.

"I saw this cool card trick," I said quickly. "This little kid did it. It was about four burglars."

"Ah," Harry said with a grin. He was keeping an eye on me, avoiding the gaze of people passing by. "The Four Burglars. A classic."

Although the trick had looked pretty simple, I couldn't figure out how the kid had done it. He had four Jacks and placed three of them in different places in a deck of cards. And then, with a simple tap of his finger on the top of the deck, all the Jacks returned to the top.

It really puzzled me.

"How did it work?"

"How do you think it worked?"

"I don't know," I said. That's why I was asking him. Sometimes talking to Uncle Harry could be a little frustrating. I'd ask a question. He'd respond with a question. Getting a real answer could sometimes take a while.

"Keep thinking on it," Harry said.

We made our way out of the crowded Dealers Room and into the lobby. Although it was also filled with magicians, the lobby felt less cramped than the room we'd just left.

"We'll head back to the Dealers Room when the crowd thins out a bit," Harry said. "I don't know about you two, but I could do with some lunch."

That sounded good to me. But before we could pick a restaurant destination, there was suddenly another person in front of us who wanted to talk to Harry. He was wearing a badge like Harry's, which meant he was one of the other conference organizers.

"Harry, there's a bit of a brouhaha bubbling over there," the older man said as he pointed to the other side of the lobby.

"Really?" Harry said. "What's the issue?"

"It's Aaron Sims. And Davis McKenzie."

"Oh dear," Harry said quietly. "Davis McKenzie. I'll go see if I can prevent a full-blown explosion."

He headed across the lobby as Nathan and I followed. I ran to catch up with him.

"Who's Davis McKenzie?" I asked. "And Aaron Sims?"

"Aaron Sims is a fine magician, a smart creator, and someone who would never claim another person's work as his own."

"And who is Davis McKenzie?"

"He's just the opposite."

A SMALL CROWD HAD GATHERED AROUND THE two men, who appeared to be in the midst of a heated argument. Uncle Harry pushed his way through the crowd; Nathan and I followed, scampering through the hole he'd conveniently made for us.

"All right, fellows, let's calm down," Harry said, speaking louder than I'd ever heard him speak. The crowd—and the two men—quieted immediately. "Now what's going on here?"

"McKenzie's trying to steal my idea," said one of the two men. He was very thin and pale, with whisps of hair covering his large head. I guessed he must be Aaron Sims.

"On the contrary," the other man barked. He was a large man, with a full beard and a booming voice. "Sims refuses to recognize that I had the idea first."

This produced another burst of outrage from Sims and the two men began to yell again.

Harry waved his arms to calm them down. "Okay, okay, let's back up boys. Let's just back everything up. What's going on?"

"I made the mistake of mentioning an idea I have for a routine," Sims said, still stuttering from anger. "Something truly original."

"Not original at all," McKenzie snapped. "I had the same idea three years ago."

"So he claims," Sims snarled.

"So I <u>proved</u>," McKenzie retorted. He turned to Harry. "I told Sims I'd written up my notes for that same idea three years ago. To prove it, I went up to my hotel room to get my laptop. The idea has been sitting in a document in my Ideas Folder forever. And I proved it!"

McKenzie pointed at an open Mac laptop computer, which sat on a small table between the two men. Harry leaned down and scanned the document quickly. He looked up at Sims.

"Does this essentially describe your idea?" Harry asked.

Sims nodded, but I could tell it was killing him. "Yes. But he had plenty of time while he was in his room to quickly type up my idea so he could call it his own. Which is what I think he did."

"Look at the document," McKenzie countered. "Click on "Get Info." It will prove that I wrote this three years ago."

Harry looked at the laptop and then turned to me

and Nathan. "I haven't got my glasses, Eli. Can you check this, confirm what he's saying?"

Nathan and I stepped forward. I clicked "Get Info" on the document. Nathan and I scanned the information.

"It says it was created about three years ago," I said to Harry.

"And saved at the same time," Nathan added.

"You see!" McKenzie snarled. "I was telling the truth."

"That would be a first," Sims replied. "You had more than enough time while you were in your room to re-set the clock on your computer. Set it for three years ago. Quickly type up what I had said. Then save it and reset the clock to today's date."

Harry turned to me and Nathan. We nodded.

"He could have done that," I said. "The problem is, there would be no way to prove it."

"Actually, Eli," Nathan said as he turned back to the laptop and studied the screen. "There might be one way to prove it."

HOW DOES NATHAN THINK HE CAN PROVE THE DOCUMENT WASN'T WRITTEN THREE YEARS AGO?

"WHAT DO YOU MEAN NATHAN?" HARRY
asked.

"It was something you said before," Nathan said
slowly. "When you told everyone to back up."

"Interesting," Harry said. "And how does that
apply?"

"Well, if he did what he's being accused of,"
Nathan continued. "If he backdated the computer and
<u>then</u> created the document, then the meta data would
always show that it was written and saved three years
ago."

"Because it was," McKenzie said.

Harry hushed him. "But if that's not true, how do
we prove it?"

"The computer could prove it for us," Nathan
said. "This is a Mac laptop, which comes with a built-
in back-up application. Lots of computers come with
them now, standard. On the Mac, it's called Time
Machine. I noticed the icon at the top of the screen
when we were checking the information on that
document."

Nathan turned to the laptop and moved the cursor
up to a small clock at the top of the screen. "Time

Machine backs up the hard drive at regular intervals, as long as you attach an exterior drive to it. But even if you don't, it still always has the most recent back-up, from the last week or so."

He clicked on the clock icon. A new folder popped open on the screen.

"This is the automated back-up from last week," Nathan said. "So, if he actually created the document three years ago, it's been saved every week along with everything else in his Ideas folder. Let's see if it's in the version of that folder from a week ago."

Nathan clicked a couple of times, opening the previous week's back-up. He then opened a folder called Ideas.

"Although the document appears in today's version of that folder, it isn't in last week's version of the folder," Nathan said. He looked up at Harry. "Which means he wrote the document at some point after this most recent back-up."

"The kid doesn't know what he's talking about," McKenzie hissed.

"On the contrary. He may be speaking well over my head, but the proof is in the pudding," Harry said. He pointed at the laptop's screen. "Your document was not in your Ideas folder a week ago. I think this is what they call being caught dead to rights."

With that, Harry snapped the laptop lid closed and handed the computer to McKenzie. "I would suggest that you take your computer and find the nearest exit," Harry said firmly. "Before hotel security does it for you."

McKenzie did what he was told, muttering as he stormed away, his laptop jammed up under his arm. He turned back and scowled at us one last time before disappearing into the crowd of magicians.

"HERE'S WHAT YOU TWO NEED TO KNOW about magicians," Harry said. He wiped a small glob of ketchup from the edge of his mouth. "Although they are a unique class, they share one factor along with all other humans."

He had taken the two of us to lunch at the hotel coffee shop. Nathan and I each ordered cheeseburgers and malts. Harry did the same, but said if anyone asked, we should say he'd ordered a salad. I think the "anyone" he meant was Aunt Alice.

"What's that one shared factor?" I asked. I slurped the last of my malt through my straw.

"With all humans, there are a small percentage who are saints. A larger percentage who do the best they can. And then another small percentage who are just no darned good at all. Those same percentages apply, for better or for worse, to the classification known as magicians."

Nathan and I nodded at this and then continued to eat in silence.

"How are you two enjoying the magic convention so far?" Harry said.

"It's really interesting," Nathan said.

I nodded. "It's sort of inspirational. In a weird way. And it's also not."

Harry leaned forward. "How do you mean, Eli?"

"Well, it's inspirational, because I'm seeing lots of kids older than me who seem to know less about magic than I do. But then it's sort of anti-inspirational, because I'm also seeing kids who are younger than me who know tons more than I know about magic. Like that little kid who did the burglar trick."

"Eli, you've stumbled onto a problem which every magician must face," Harry said with a chuckle. "There are always going to be people who know more than you do on the subject. And there are always going to be people who know less. Judging yourself based on either metric is clearly a waste of your time."

I thought about this as I finished my fries. "I've

been thinking about how that burglar trick might have been done," I said.

"Me too," Nathan added.

"And what have you come up with?" Harry asked with a grin.

We each offered up our ideas on how the Jacks might have moved from different positions in the deck to the top in the blink of an eye.

When we'd exhausted our possible solutions, Harry leaned back and smiled at us.

"Well done, boys. Some very original thinking there. You know, my friend Dai Vernon said something interesting once," Harry said.

I remembered that name. It was the magician who Cecilia had tattooed on her arm (although it was really a temporary tattoo. And the guy was actually Walt Disney.)

"Dai said that the problem with most magicians is that they stop thinking too soon." Harry beamed at us from across the table. "I think I'm looking at two magicians who aren't going to have that problem. And, as a result, are going to go far."

He then put his napkin over his empty plate and shoved it to one side, creating a space in front of him on the table. "Now do you want me to show you the likely method that kid used to perform The Four

Burglars? In case you like it better than the options you created?"

Nathan and I nodded as Harry pulled out his ever-present deck of cards.

Although we both listened as he explained the moves in the trick, I think Nathan and I were thinking the exact same thing.

My Uncle Harry—who apparently was a pretty big deal throughout the magic world—thought that both of us were going to go far as magicians!

I couldn't help but smile.

This was turning out to be a <u>great</u> magic convention.

CHAPTER TEN

THE LAST OF CECILIA

TRADITIONALLY, the last day of school ended with an amateur talent show, which was open to all the kids.

I loved this idea. A show, followed by no more school? That's a tough combo to beat.

At Cecilia's insistence, I had agreed to join her in doing a short magic routine on stage.

I think she offered this good news in order to help take the sting out of her bad news: Cecilia and her family were moving away. Like, right away. This week.

"That's why I couldn't be at the Wizards' Week-end," she explained. "My dad is being transferred for his job. I had to fly to California with my parents to see our new house."

"Uh huh," I said quietly. I was trying to keep any and all emotion out of my voice.

We were standing in the hall outside the school auditorium, going over our magic routine one last time. The show was scheduled to start in about a half hour. I could hear the sound of kids and teachers filling up the theater.

"We'll be living only a few miles from The Magic Castle," she continued as she bent down to re-tie one of the laces of her bright red high-top sneakers. "Although I'm too young to get into The Magic Castle —except for the Sunday Brunch—I'm hoping to be able to join their Junior Program," she continued as she gave the lace one final tug.

"That would be cool," I said as flatly as possible. Before I could ask for more detail, we were interrupted by a voice coming down the hall.

"Cecilia, can I talk to you for a moment?" It was Mrs. Katz, who had directed the school play. She was also in charge of the talent show.

"Sure thing," Cecilia said.

"We've run into a bit of a problem," Mrs. Katz said. She turned and glanced down the hall, where I could see a man standing. He was silhouetted by a large window. His shape looked vaguely familiar.

"What's up?" Cecilia said.

"Well, the thing is, we've always billed this show as an amateur talent contest," Mrs. Katz began. She sounded like she was having trouble finding the words she wanted to say. "And it's come to our attention that you aren't—strictly speaking—an amateur. I understand you've been paid on more than one occasion to perform magic. At birthday parties."

"I have indeed," Cecilia said with pride. "Four so far. Each and every one of them a hit."

"I don't doubt that," Mrs. Katz said, trying to smile. "However, since we've billed this as an amateur talent show, one of the parents has objected to allowing a professional into the mix."

"What does that mean? Because I got paid, I can't do the show?" Cecilia said. She was clearly upset with this news. I was upset, too, but I was also still reeling from Cecilia's news about moving away.

"I'm sorry, but I think it would set a bad precedent," Mrs. Katz said. She turned again to glance at the man down the hall.

It was then that I recognized him: It was Mr. Hartwell, father of Simon Hartwell.

Cecilia must have recognized him as well.

"Does this have anything to do with the fact that Simon Hartwell entered the talent contest with the intention of performing magic?" Cecilia asked. She had gone from heartbroken to angry in a split second. "And he didn't want to compete against us?"

"I really can't speak to that," Mrs. Katz said. "You can take this issue up with the School Board at the next meeting, of course."

"And when do they meet next?"

"In August."

Cecilia shook her head. "Fat lot of good that will do."

"I'm sorry Cecilia," Mrs. Katz said. "And I'm sorry Eli."

"No need to apologize to Eli," Cecilia said suddenly. "There's nothing saying he can't perform today."

"No, I suppose there isn't," Mrs. Katz agreed. "Good luck, Eli. You better take your place backstage. The show's about to start."

And with that she was gone.

I turned to Cecilia as she pulled open the door to the backstage area.

"Are you crazy? I can't perform. If we're not doing the act we rehearsed, I don't have anything to do."

She gave me a gentle shove, pushing me through the door into the darkness.

"You'll think of something. I have complete faith in you," she said.

And then the door swung shut.

That's nice, I thought. She has faith in me.

It would be great if I had some faith in myself as well.

ALL THE PERFORMERS MINGLED BACKSTAGE, quietly whispering and laughing nervously, waiting for the show to start.

The whole backstage area was bathed in a blue light, in sharp contrast to the bright white lights on the stage. Standing in the wings, I could see the principal —Mr. Moore—as he welcomed the audience with a few lame jokes.

I stepped away, moving deeper into the blue-tinted darkness, racking my brain to come up with something I could do. The good news (and oddly enough, also the bad news) was that I was scheduled to be the last act in the show.

So, I had time. Plenty of time.

Just no ideas.

"What? Are you flying solo today, Marks?"

I turned to see Simon Hartwell. He was dressed in a tacky tux and carried a suitcase. On the side of the case was a professionally printed sign. It read: "Simon

Says ... Abracadabra!" along with a silhouette of a magician in a top hat.

He didn't bother to wait for a response, just kept walking. He set the case down next to the award table. He flipped the case open and started organizing his props. He glanced up at me and then up at the three golden award statues on the table.

"Feast your eyes on the prize now, Marks," Simon said with a greasy grin. "Because one of those babies is coming home with me, not you. Probably the top prize."

Clearly he knew that Cecilia had been pulled from the show. And this fact was making him more annoyingly confident than usual.

I turned and tried to ignore him. I had to think of something I could perform. And I needed to think of it quickly.

I pulled my constant companions—a deck of playing cards—from my pocket. I began to sort through the cards, hoping they might inspire a good idea. Or any idea.

But then I stopped sorting.

The cards looked strange.

There were no red suits—hearts and diamonds. All the pips were black. Black spades and clubs. I looked closer. And also black hearts and black diamonds. Was I going nuts?

Then I figured it out. It was the blue light which bathed the backstage. It made the red colors on the cards look black.

Good thing that wouldn't be an issue on stage; under the white lights, all the cards would look normal.

I peeked out from behind the curtain. The first act was up: A girl was twirling a baton to a disco song. The song was called *I Will Survive*. I watched for several seconds. She didn't seem to have great control of the baton, which she whirled at high speed over her head. I hoped the song was making the correct prediction about the girl and the outcome of her act.

I turned toward the audience. I couldn't see anything beyond the front row, just a sea of darkness. But I'd seen *"Oliver!"* in this theater. I knew that it seated several hundred people. There was no way that a simple card trick was going to be seen by a crowd this size.

I put the cards away and continued to pace under the hazy blue lights.

I DIDN'T REALLY PAY ATTENTION TO THE NEXT half dozen acts. Instead, I mentally ran through all the tricks I'd learned (or seen or read about) over the last nine months.

Nothing was jumping out at me as being the ideal trick for this situation.

My growing panic was interrupted by the sound of laughter. Genuine, outright, prolonged laughter.

I peeked through the curtain.

The current performer was Jake North, the kid who had played Fagin in *"Oliver!"* He had a friend playing the piano and Jake was singing short bits of different songs. In-between each verse, he'd stop singing and do a quick impression of one of the teachers. That impression would lead into the next bit of a song, which he'd re-written to make it somehow about that teacher.

He was making fun of the teachers. And the crowd was loving it.

I got caught up in his act for several seconds. As he had proven in the play, Jake was a really good performer.

When he finished his act, I forced myself to return to my backstage pacing. I needed to come up with a short magic trick that would work in front of a large audience.

CHAPTER TEN

The next performer was Simon Hartwell. As far as I could tell, he appeared to be the only other person who was doing magic. I knew I should spend the precious time I had left coming up with an idea. Instead, I decided to at least take a quick look at my competition.

He was terrible.

I'm not just saying that because I didn't like him. He was objectively terrible.

I'd heard a few speeches from Uncle Harry over the last few months about the things magicians *shouldn't* do while performing.

And it felt like Simon was doing all of them.

He started with a coin trick, which was lost in front of the large audience.

He called someone on-stage as a volunteer and then basically made fun of them. ("Give me your hand. No, your *clean* hand. Oh, I guess that was your clean hand.")

He tried to make the volunteer look foolish. But he was so mean about it that—in only a few seconds—he had the whole crowd turned against him.

His act went from bad to worse. His father had clearly bought a bunch of expensive tricks for him, and Simon barely knew how to use any of them.

For a few moments, I almost felt sorry for Simon.

He was sweating and looked miserable as he struggled to finish his magic act. It wasn't a long act, but it felt like it went on forever.

And I bet it seemed even longer to Simon.

I'd heard Uncle Harry's friend Max Monarch describe an act he'd seen as "swirling down the toilet of despair." And I finally knew what Max meant.

Simon Hartwell and his act were swirling down the toilet of despair.

And at that instant, I suddenly knew exactly what I should do for my performance.

AFTER PRINCIPAL MOORE INTRODUCED ME, I was surprised at how calm I was as I walked out onstage into the super bright lights.

I really had no right to be.

I was about to perform a trick I'd never done before. That was the golden rule in magic: Never, ever do a trick for an audience until you've practiced it until it's beyond perfect. And I was breaking that rule. Shattering it, actually.

Although I had never done the trick, I had seen it. Several hundred times.

There were two videotapes in Uncle Harry's library I had watched over and over again.

One was of a magician couple—called The Pendragons—and an act they did called *Metamorphosis*. She got into a big canvas bag and went into a trunk. He got on top of the trunk. He pulled a sheet up, covering himself for a split second. Then he dropped the sheet. But it was no longer him. <u>She</u> was standing on the trunk. And <u>he</u> was discovered inside the trunk. And also inside the canvas bag.

Incredible.

And impossible for me to do, even if Cecilia was still here.

However, the other trick I watched over and over <u>was</u> something I could do.

Maybe not as well as the magician on the videotape. But I could do it.

I only needed a volunteer.

"Thanks for that introduction, Principal Moore. Do you mind joining me on-stage for a moment?"

I had learned from Jake's act that the audience liked it when the teachers were involved.

And I had learned from Simon's act that—until proven otherwise—the audience was always going to be on the side of the volunteer.

I had brought out a chair and I gestured to Principal Moore that he should take a seat in it.

"You once gave me a terrific piece of advice," I began. "I had been sent to your office. It was the second day of school. I was off to a great start."

This line got me my first laugh. Even Principal Moore laughed.

"You gave me some smart advice," I continued. "I had been practicing a magic move in class and I kept dropping coins. And you said, 'Eli, you need to get quieter coins.'"

This produced another laugh.

"So, I switched to something that would make a little less noise. Something softer."

I picked up a roll of toilet paper I had stashed behind the chair.

This got a huge laugh. And I was off and running.

On Harry's old videotape, I had seen a magician named Slydini perform this trick hundreds of times. He would take a crushed-up tissue and make it vanish in front of the volunteer's eyes. Again and again and again.

What the volunteer didn't realize—but the audience did—was that Slydini wasn't making the balls disappear. He was merely tossing the balls of tissues over the volunteer's head, just out of their line of sight.

Again and again and again.

I can't say that I did the trick as well as Slydini did.

I didn't.

But I did it well enough to get a lot of laughs from the crowd. And a big round of applause at the end. That was when I made the roll of toilet paper disappear in front of Principal Moore's eyes (by tossing it over his head!).

I left the stage feeling elated and a little exhausted. And realizing one surprising fact: As crazy as the whole thing had been, I had loved every minute of it.

"Everyone did a wonderful job this afternoon," Principal Moore said from the center of the stage. He unfolded a piece of paper. "It's my great pleasure to announce our top three winners of this year's Amateur Talent Contest."

I was seated in the front row with all the other contestants. I turned and could see Nathan a few rows back. He gave me a big thumbs up. I scanned the crowd and finally spotted Cecilia. She was standing off to the side, leaning against the wall. I think if I hadn't been performing, she might have skipped the show altogether. She too gave me a thumbs up, followed by a big smile.

Principal Moore was suddenly interrupted by Mrs. Katz, who ran on-stage, looking perplexed. She glanced around the stage and then turned to the Principal.

"They're gone. Someone stole the prize statues."

This produced a sudden gasp in the crowd, followed by lots of murmuring.

"Are you sure?" Principal Moore asked.

"They're not there," Mrs. Katz huffed. "Someone stole them."

"And that someone was Cecilia Hernandez!" came a voice from the front row.

I looked over and saw it was Simon Hartwell.

"I saw her take them," Simon continued as he stood up and pointed at her.

"Simon, that's quite the accusation," Principal Moore said. "Can you back that up?"

"I sure can," he said confidently. "After I finished my routine, I was on the floor by the award table, putting my props away into my suitcase. Someone walked by the table, and I know it was Cecilia. I recognized her bright red sneakers. I was surprised, because I knew she had been kicked out of the show. And then, after I closed my suitcase, I stood up and noticed that the award statues were gone. I think she was getting back at you for cutting her from the show."

"That's a lie," Cecilia shouted from her position by the wall.

"Cecilia, we will deal with this later. In my office," Mr. Moore said.

"You don't have to wait," I said as I jumped up. "Simon is lying. And I can prove it!"

HOW CAN ELI PROVE THAT SIMON IS LYING?

"THERE WAS NO WAY SIMON COULD HAVE SEEN Cecilia's red sneakers backstage," I explained.

It was later that night, and I was recounting the events of the day to Uncle Harry and Aunt Alice over dinner.

"Why was that dear?" Aunt Alice asked.

"Because the whole backstage area was bathed in blue light," I explained. "That made everything that was red look black. I'd noticed the effect when I was sorting through my playing cards."

"So, Simon couldn't identify Cecilia's red sneakers, because her shoes—like everything else red—would have appeared black under the blue lights," Harry said. "The thief could just have easily been someone with black sneakers. Or green for that matter. They'll all look black under a blue light."

"Interesting," Aunt Alice said. "So did Simon own up to his lie?"

"Better than that," I said with a grin. "They went through his prop case and found he had used it to hide the awards. I guess he knew there was no chance he'd ever win any of them legitimately. His act was ... bad."

"Worse than that, he made the entire field of magic

look bad," Uncle Harry added. "Which is a greater sin."

I turned to him. "You were there?"

Harry shrugged. "I might have snuck in and seen a bit of the show." He smiled at me. "Eli, you were wonderful. Slydini himself would have been proud."

"Thanks, but I know I broke the golden rule: I performed a magic trick before I'd practiced it to death. If I had, maybe I'd have won first place, instead of second. Instead of Jake North. Although, he was very good."

"There will be other shows," Aunt Alice said quietly.

"Speaking of shows, I had a call in the shop today," Harry said suddenly. "Someone looking for a young magician to perform at a kid's birthday party next month. I had a recommendation for them."

I shook my head sadly. "But Cecilia won't be able to do it. She'll be moved to California by then. She'll be gone."

"Oh, we haven't seen the last of that girl," Harry said with a grin. "But Cecilia wasn't the young magician I recommended for that birthday party."

It took several seconds longer than it should have for me to understand what he was saying.

"Me?"

Harry nodded. "I think you're ready. Of course, the downside is that, as a professional, you'll no longer be able to enter amateur talent shows."

"I think I can live with that."

He reached over to the nearby kitchen counter. "Now, I've always maintained that the best marketing you can do is to put on a great show. Word of mouth is your friend. But it never hurts to have a little something to make it easier for potential customers to track you down."

Harry held out a small cardboard box. I opened it, to find that it was filled with a tight row of business cards. I took one out and read it.

"Really?" I said as I looked up at him.

"Yes, Eli. I believe so," he said with a smile. I turned to Aunt Alice, who was also smiling at me.

And then I looked down at the card again, to make sure I'd gotten it right.

It read: *Eli Marks. Professional Magician.*

And I couldn't help but smile as well.

Eli Marks
Professional Magician
(612) 555-5603

POSTSCRIPT

NOT LONG AFTER the talent show, I received a postcard. This was the first time I'd ever received any mail since moving in with Aunt Alice and Uncle Harry.

But that's not why I saved it for years.

GREETINGS FROM
THE MAGIC CASTLE

On the front of the postcard, there was a picture of a large, impressive castle-like building. The words "Greetings from The Magic Castle" spanned most of the card.

I turned it over and read:

"Hey Eli. We are getting settled in just fine. I've been to The Magic Castle twice! You will love it! Have learned a ton of new stuff. But that's not the best news. Can't wait to share it with you."

It was signed *Cecilia*.

And beneath her name she wrote three final and very intriguing words:

"To be continued ..."

HARRY'S MAGIC
EMPORIUM

TEN FUN MAGIC TRICKS FOR YOU TO LEARN

Many of the magic tricks mentioned in the previous stories are all tricks you can easily learn at home. Eli's uncle, Harry Marks, wrote a classic book filled with magic tricks: "Harry's Magic Emporium."

Although the book has been out of print for years, Harry has graciously allowed us to re-print ten of those tricks, to help you get started in magic.

So, let's dive in and learn some tricks!

"A treasure trove of magic tricks that are easy to learn,
but will leave you audience stunned.
This is a must-have for any aspiring magician."
Max Monarch
HARRY'S
MAGIC
EMPORIUM
HARRY MARKS

THE FRENCH DROP

THE FRENCH DROP has been around forever; no one is really sure who invented it. References to similar illusions have appeared as early as the 1500s.

THE EFFECT

The French Drop is a magic move where you make a coin or other small object seem to vanish from your hands.

HOW TO DO IT

The secret to the trick is that you actually keep the coin in one of your hands, but the audience doesn't realize that you're hiding it. With some practice, you can become a master of this trick and use other techniques to make it even more convincing!

The key word though is PRACTICE!

Here's how you perform The French Drop.

Grasp a quarter or larger coin between your thumb and middle two fingers, with your palm facing upwards.

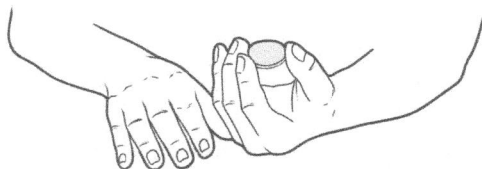

When I do this trick, I start with the coin in my left hand and appear to grab it with the right. You can do it the other way, if swapping the hands makes it easier to learn. But for these directions, we'll start with the coin being held by the thumb and first finger of your left hand.

Make sure your audience can see the coin clearly, with both hands open to prove to your audience that you have nothing hidden in either hand. Holding the coin between your thumb and middle two fingers positions it for falling directly into finger palm position.

Tilting your hand forward, ostensibly to display the coin, also aids in this.

If you don't have a coin, a small ball or similarly sized object can be used as a substitute.

Using your right hand, pretend to grab the coin. As you make that motion, let the coin fall back into your left palm. If your hand is tilted up so the coin is parallel to the floor, the coin will fall into your left palm. But by tilting your hand forward, letting go with your left thumb will allow the coin to drop into finger palm position.

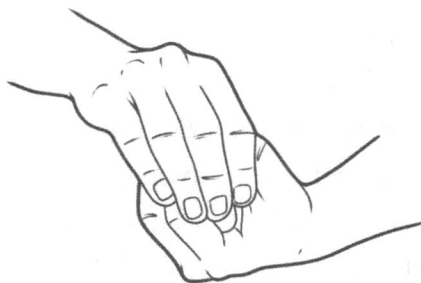

**What they don't see when you cover the
coin with your right hand:
You drop the coin into your palm.**

As you close your left hand around the dropped coin, pull your right hand away, acting as if you've grabbed the coin with that hand.

This is the part you'll have to work on the most. The acting is half the illusion with The French Drop.

The real secret of this trick is to keep your eyes on your right hand as it moves away. That's what helps to sell the illusion. You can even lower your left hand to your side to keep them from watching it. The key is, don't draw attention to your left hand by looking at it.

With all the focus on your right hand, make a magic gesture (rub your fingers together or blow on the right hand or even pass the left hand over it) and then slowly peel back each of the fingers of the right hand to reveal that the coin has disappeared!

You are then open to reveal the missing coin in any manner you like, such as appearing to pull it from your elbow or from behind a subject's ear.

Like I said earlier, this one takes PRACTICE to really master.

COIN THROUGH TABLE (NOT)

COIN THROUGH TABLE (Not) is a fun trick which can be done just about anywhere you've got a table, a napkin, a coin, a saltshaker ... and an audience.

Again, it's one of those tricks where no one is entirely certain who first created it. However, references to similar tricks date as far back as the book *The Discoverie of Witchcraft*, back in 1584!

THE EFFECT

You explain that many tables have weak spots, where less-dense materials can easily pass through them.

A coin is placed on the table and covered with a saltshaker. The shaker is then covered with a napkin.

You slam your hand down on the covered napkin and a thud is heard beneath the table.

You pull back the napkin, to reveal the coin is still there, but the saltshaker is gone.

When your audience looks under the table, they'll find that the saltshaker has passed through the table and is now resting on the floor.

SOME CONSIDERATIONS

When setting up the trick, keep a couple things in mind:

-You need to be seated, in a position where you can secretly drop the saltshaker into your lap. A tablecloth in this situation can really be your friend.

-Your audience should be seated across from you; otherwise, you might flash the drop to people seated on either side of you. *("Flash" means that something you want to be hidden can be spotted by a spectator.)*

-The napkin you use must be thick enough that we can't see through it. It also needs to be thick enough (and pliable enough) that it will maintain the shape of the saltshaker even after you've ditched it. If you're using a paper napkin, you may want to put two napkins together.

-Make sure the saltshaker you're using can survive a

short drop to the floor. So, this might not be the best trick to employ Grandma's antique crystal saltshaker.

How To Do It

Place a coin near the center of the table. Maybe slide it around until you find the best spot.

"*Not a lot of people know this, but just about any table has a weak spot in it. A spot that's not as solid as the rest of the table. Some spots are so weak, you can actually push a small object through the table. Let me demonstrate.*"

Place a saltshaker on top of the coin.

"*We'll need something a little larger to push the coin*

through the table. And just so I don't make a mess, let's cover the saltshaker."

Drape a napkin over the saltshaker, grasping it tightly, so that the napkin takes on the shape of the saltshaker.

Pull the draped saltshaker back as you point at the coin.

"As you can see, the coin is resting comfortably atop the table. But not for long!"

While you're talking about the coin, secretly drop the saltshaker into your lap. Make sure the napkin maintains the shape of the saltshaker.

Place the napkin (still in the shape of the salt-shaker) over the coin.

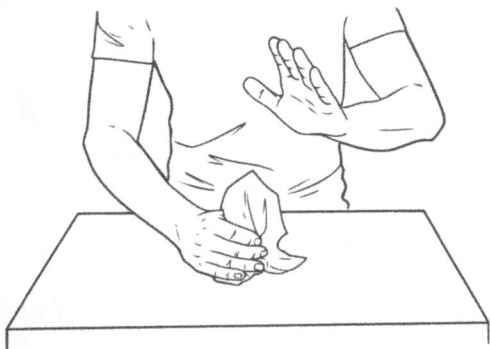

"Let's see if I've found the right spot."

With the palm of your hand, slam the napkin down onto the tabletop. At the same time, open your legs and let the saltshaker drop to the floor.

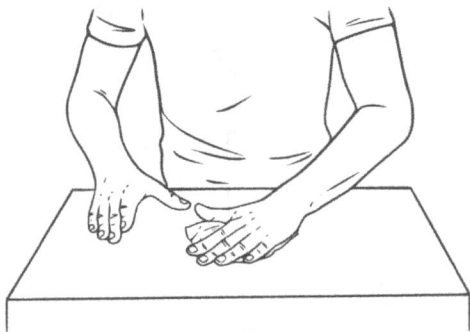

Pull back the napkin to reveal the saltshaker is gone, but the coin is still there.

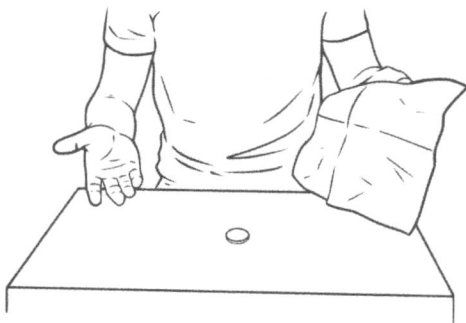

"Oh dear, looks like the coin was stronger than the table ... but it was the saltshaker that was the weaker object! Do you mind grabbing the saltshaker for me?"

Your audience member looks under the table, surprised to see the saltshaker is now laying on the floor.

NOTE: This trick can be done with objects other than a saltshaker; anything whose shape can be draped and masked by the napkin (and that will survive a drop to the floor). You can also do the trick without the coin, simply using the saltshaker itself as the object that passes through the table.

HYPNO-KNEE

THIS IS a fun illusion which employs some little-known principles of human physiology and kinesiology. It's a surprising effect, which I first learned from my pal Walter Gibson. He published it as "A Weak Knee" in his books *Secrets of Magic* in 1946 and *The Complete Beginner's Guide to Magic* in 1997.

You can do this trick in front of a crowd, a small group or just for one friend.

THE EFFECT

You explain that you're learning hypnosis, and although you're not good enough to hypnotize a whole person (yet!), you <u>can</u> do various limbs.

You ask your volunteer to stand next to a wall and explain that you're going to hypnotize their knee.

You make some magical gestures around their left knee and then ask them to lift their left leg off the floor.

They won't be able to do it!

How To Do It

Start by explaining that you've been studying hypnosis, but that you're just a beginner.

"I can't do a whole person yet, but I can do a knee. Let me show you."

Ask your volunteer to stand next to a wall.

Then instruct them: *"Place your right foot against the wall, with your left foot about six inches away from the right."*

Once they're in position, wave your hands by their left knee, telling the knee that it is getting sleepy. You can really ham it up here, if you want.

After several seconds of this, step back and instruct

your volunteer to—without moving any other part of their body—lift their left leg off the floor.

Once it's clear they can't do it, reverse your hypnotic spell.

"Your knee is now awake. Step forward, first with your right foot, to make sure your left leg can support you."

Your volunteer should have no trouble walking toward you.

And they'll have no idea how you were able to hypnotize their knee!

BANANA SPLIT

I KNOW your parents always told you not to play with your food. But it's okay just this once!

You can find a more elaborate version of this trick in *Tarbell, Volume One (Bewitched Banana)*. However, I prefer this (apparently) impromptu version, because when it's performed properly it really does feel like magic. And audience members, thinking back on it, will simply not be able to figure out how you managed the trick!

THE EFFECT

You offer to share your unpeeled banana with two or three friends.

Using your magical powers, you slice the banana into even segments—just by pointing at it, without even needing to peel it.

When the banana is finally peeled, it's revealed that it is already perfectly sliced into three (or four) segments!

How To Do It

This trick takes just a bit of preparation, away from prying eyes.

You'll need a banana (obviously) and a needle or long, thin pin. The needle/pin can't be too thick.

First, determine how many segments you want to divide the banana into. For our purposes, we'll say you want four pieces.

Make sure your needle/pin is long enough to go in one side of the banana and <u>nearly</u> come out the other.

(You can measure your pin against the side of the banana to be sure.)

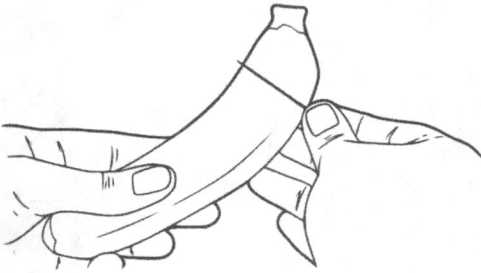

Pick a point near the top of the banana, where the first slice would end if the banana were peeled. Push the needle or pin into the banana, toward the other side (without breaking through on the other side).

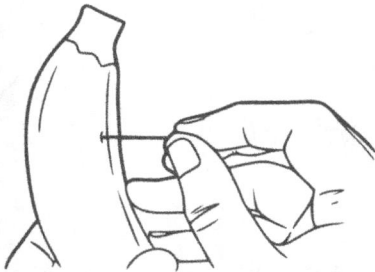

Move the needle/pin from side to side, slicing through the banana's interior.

Pull the needle/pin out and pick another point further down the banana (about the length of the next segment). Repeat the process outlined above, pushing the needle/pin into the banana and moving it from side to side.

You'll need to repeat the process, doing it one less time than the number of finished segments you want (for example, do it twice for three segments, three times for four segments, and so on).

WITH THE BANANA THUS PREPARED, YOU'RE now ready to perform the trick.

"I like bananas, but don't feel like eating the whole thing. Can I share it with the three of you?"

Adjust the wording to fit the number of people and the number of segments.

"To keep things hygienic, I'll slice it into segments

<u>before</u> *I peel it. Let's see, I need (counting), looks like four segments."*

Use a magical gesture to mime cutting the banana into four slices. You can also use a knife, waving it over the banana but never touching it. Or like in the Tarbell version, you can use a playing card to mime sawing through the banana.

"There we go: All sliced and ready to eat."

Peel the banana, proving that it is in fact already cut into the predicted number of segments.

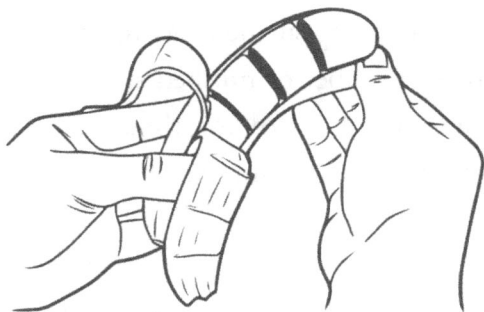

NOTE: To help hide the two (or three or four) pin pricks in the banana, don't do them in a straight line. Instead, rotate the banana during that process, so the nearly invisible pin pricks aren't all in a straight line.

THE RISING CARD

The Rising Card Trick, in various forms, has been around for hundreds of years. There are nearly as many variations on how to do it as there are magicians who perform it. One version is detailed in *Modern Magic* (1876).

The nice thing about this version you're about to read, is that as you begin to learn more about card magic (such as how to force cards and do false shuffles), you can add flourishes to this basic routine. But even a beginner can produce a magical result with just a little practice.

The Effect

The effect itself is pretty straightforward: a participant selects a random card. You return the card to the deck and put the deck back into the box. Then, after some magical incantations, their chosen card magically rises up out of the card box.

How To Do It

This trick requires a little arts and crafts work at home before you can get started.

You'll need to cut a hole on the front of the card box (you want the side where the box top is attached, not the side where the flap opens).

This hole goes from the bottom of the box up toward the top and should be about three-quarters of an inch wide.

Now you're ready to perform the trick.

Take the deck of cards out of the box, making sure

your audience doesn't ever see the side of the box with a hole in it.

Ask the participant to pick a card.

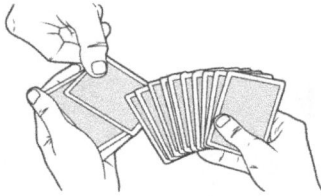

Take their chosen card and return it to the top of the deck, by any means you prefer. This can be as simple as putting it on the top of the deck ... or using some sleight of hand to get it to the top of the deck. But for starting out, just putting it on the top of the deck will be fine.

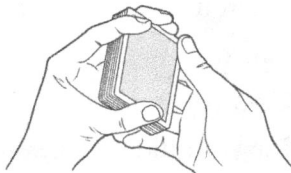

Put the deck of cards back in the box. Make sure the faces of the cards are toward the solid side of the card box — the side without the hole cut in it.

Now it's time for you to be imaginative and have some fun: You need to create a reason why their card rises out of the box.

-Have you hypnotized the card?

-Are you and your participant using your combined psychic energy to make the card rise?

-Is the card thankful that the participant picked it and it wants to rejoin its new master? (Like a dog who comes when it's called.)

Whatever reason you come up with, you will make that card rise, using your index finger and that hole you cut. You'll be moving the playing card closest to the hole, which—if you did it correctly—is the top card in the deck.

Push against that card with your finger, pushing upward ... and their chosen card will start to rise ...

Your Point of View

Your Point of View

Until it is revealed to be their chosen card!

You can hand it out if you wish or move on to the next trick.

Just MAKE SURE they NEVER see the side of the box that has the hole in it!

DANCING HANKY

This is a funny, impromptu trick you can do on a moment's notice, using your own hanky or even borrowing one from a volunteer. I always use my own hanky, because after some experimenting, I finally found one that was the right thickness for my purposes. You may want to do some sampling of your own to find one that works best for you.

THE EFFECT

You produce a pocket handkerchief and twirl it so it's like a short, tight piece of rope. Using your magical powers, you make the handkerchief stand up, take a bow and move back in forth, like it has a mind of its own. You then attach an "invisible" thread to the upper corner of the handkerchief and make the handkerchief follow your directions, even though you're not (apparently) touching it.

HOW TO DO IT

Hold the handkerchief up by the two top corners (A & B).

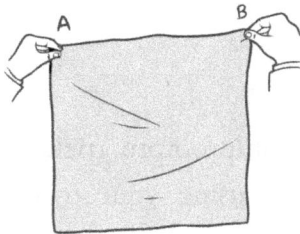

Then move your fingers down from the A corner an inch or so.

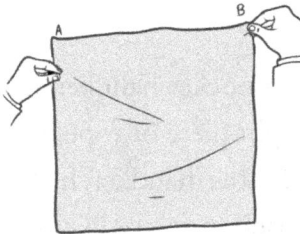

Grasping that point with two fingers on your left hand (and grasping the B corner with two fingers on your right hand), twirl the handkerchief until it becomes long and rope-like.

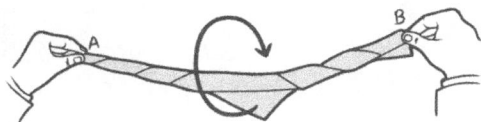

(*NOTE: Gripping from both corners, A & B, would create a less strong coil in the center of the handkerchief. This impacts your ability to control the handkerchief during the routine. So always pick a point an inch or so below the A corner. It provides much more control on the rolled-up hanky. Thanks to Amazing Stephen for this tip!*)

Still in your right hand, pull the B corner up in front of you (while bringing the A corner straight down). While holding the B corner, slide your left hand up and grip the top ... and then slide your left hand down to the middle of the twisted handkerchief. Grip the middle tightly, placing your left thumb against the handkerchief.

It is your thumb which will control the movement of the Dancing Hanky, which should be able to stand up on its own without a lot of pressure from your left thumb.

You can make it dance, left and right, up and down. Make it seem like it is alive and lively. Like a happy puppy.

Then, pretend to pull a hair out of your head. (Or pretend to pull it from a volunteer's head—but be sure to pretend!) Mime wrapping this invisible hair around the top tip of the hanky.

You can now pretend to "pull" the tip of the hanky, left and right, up and down, with this invisible hair. And, by moving your thumb at the same time, it will appear that the hanky is under your control and actually being pulled by this invisible leash.

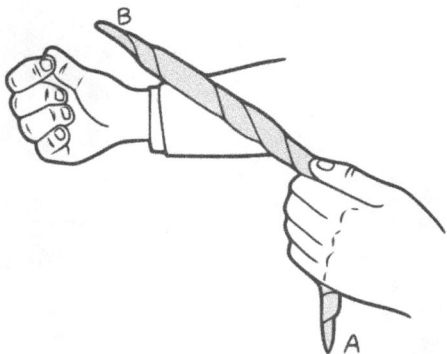

Create your own dancing routine with the hanky —use your imagination!

For a finale, crush the hanky in your hands, shake it out and return it to your pocket.

ROLLING A COIN

There are two schools of thought on flashy moves in magic. One group loves them, because it sets you—as the performer—apart from the audience by demonstrating a special and interesting skill. The other opinion is that it draws too much attention to your skill, thus making every move you make a bit suspect.

I'm really not a huge fan of flashy effects for their own sake. But I think rolling a coin across the backs of your knuckles is an exception. Not only does it demonstrate unique dexterity to your audience, but it also makes you better at handling coins. It's that simple: Spend enough time learning to roll a coin across your knuckles and you're bound to improve your overall skill at handling (and manipulating) coins.

The Effect

The performer shows off their skill as a magician by making a coin roll from finger to finger across the back of their hand.

After this amazing journey, the coin disappears beneath the fingers only to instantly reappear and go around again!

The coin really looks like it's got a life of its own as the magician keeps repeating the moves over and over.

How To Do It

First, a quick bit of terminology.

While you may know many things as well as you know the back of your hand, let's take a moment to see how well you know your actual hand.

The first drawing indicates the names we'll be using for each of your digits.

I've also put the letters "A" and "B" on the opposite edges of the coin, so you can better track its journey.

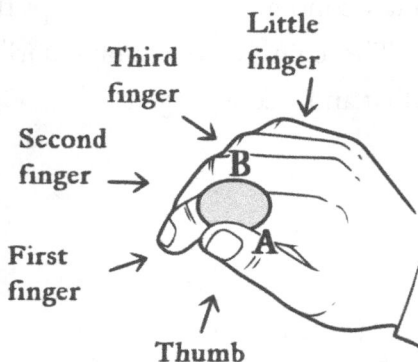

Using your thumb, push the coin up so that the coin rolls over the back of the first finger next to the knuckle. *Depending on the size of your hands, you can start with either a quarter or a fifty-cent piece. Within just a few attempts, you'll quickly figure out which one is right for you.*

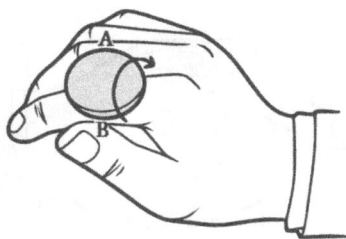

Raise your second finger so that it clips the Edge B of the coin. The coin is now momentarily clipped between the first and second fingers.

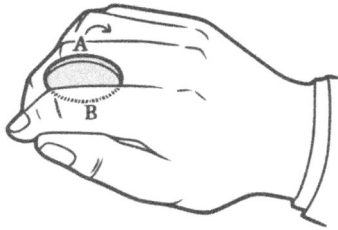

But don't stop there! Lift your first finger, pushing the coin onto the back of your second finger.

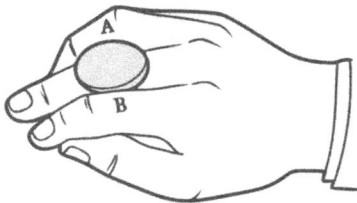

Keep things moving! Raise your third finger and grip Edge A. This permits the coin to roll over the second finger. Like before, the coin will now be momentarily wedged between your second and third fingers.

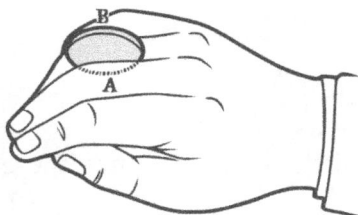

Don't stop now! With a slight tilt of your hand, the coin will then naturally tip onto the back of your third finger.

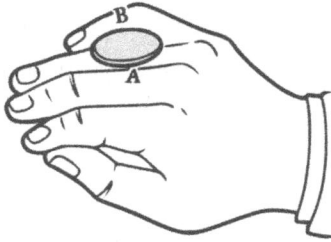

Lift your little finger and snag the Edge B of the coin. For just a moment, the coin will be wedged between your third finger and your little finger.

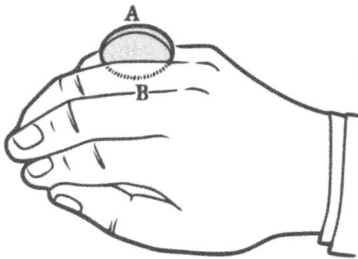

This is where it can get tricky. Adjust your little

finger, so that the little finger can move the coin through the gap between your third finger and your little finger. If done correctly, most of the coin will now be on the palm side of your hand, snagged between your third finger and your little finger.

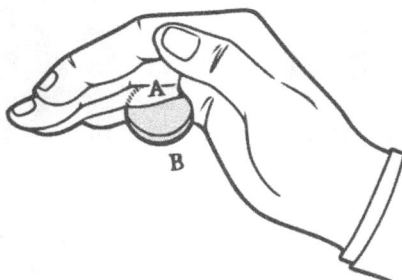

Swing your thumb across your palm so that it's right under the coin.

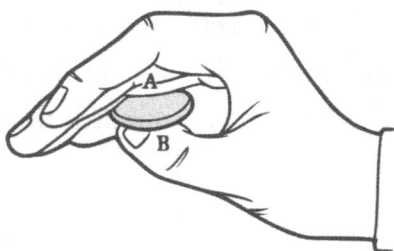

Let the coin drop onto the edge of your thumb.

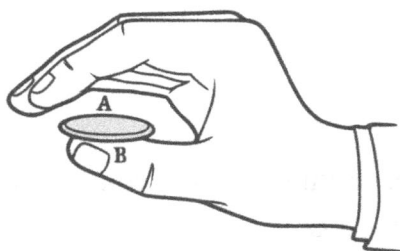

The thumb then swings over, pressing the coin against the fingers and then pushing the coin back up to the start position, right along the edge of your first finger.

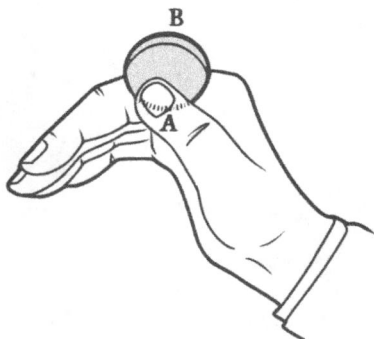

If all has gone to plan, you should be back where you started *(at the first illustration)!* You can now move the coin across the knuckle of the first finger and run through all the moves again ... ad infinitum!

This set of moves will require a lot of practice and patience on your part. However, the beauty of the effect is that you can practice it just about anywhere.

THE UNPOPPABLE BALLOON

This is one of my favorite "impossible looking" tricks that is actually quite easy to do. You can add flourishes to the end (like popping the balloon and producing some confetti or a flower) or simply present it as a magical skill.

The Effect

The magician takes a blown-up balloon and a long, thin needle (a wooden kabob skewer will do) and skillfully inserts it into the balloon. The skewer goes all the way through, until it comes out on the other side. All without popping the balloon!

How To Do It

To do this trick, you will need some clear tape, a balloon, and a kabob skewer. All of these items can be found at most grocery stores. Make sure to use clear tape that will stick nicely to the balloon.

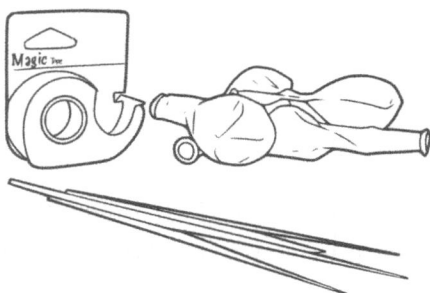

Fill a balloon to three-quarters full. Don't overfill it, as this may cause it to burst while you're doing the trick. A TIP: Longer balloons—often used for making balloon animals—don't work as well as round balloons.

DO THIS PART AWAY FROM YOUR AUDI-ENCE: Begin by placing two strips of clear tape in a cross shape anywhere on the balloon. When you're doing this trick the first few times, start by sticking the tape toward the bottom of the balloon, as this is where the rubber is less taut and so it is less likely to burst. As you become more experienced, you can try placing the cross on the sides of the balloon, where the material is more stretched.

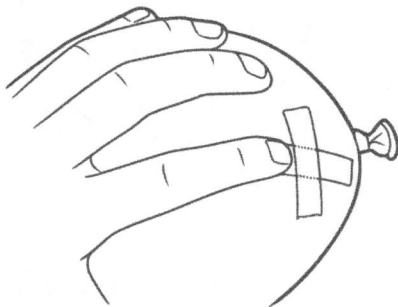

After you have put the two pieces of tape on one side of the balloon, do the same thing on the other side, directly across from the first tape cross. Make sure the two pieces of tape are directly opposite each other.

DO THIS PART IN FRONT OF YOUR AUDIENCE: Gently insert the skewer into the balloon at the middle of one of the taped crosses (the tape will keep the balloon from popping). If it does pop, try again, and make sure the tape is stuck properly to the balloon's surface.

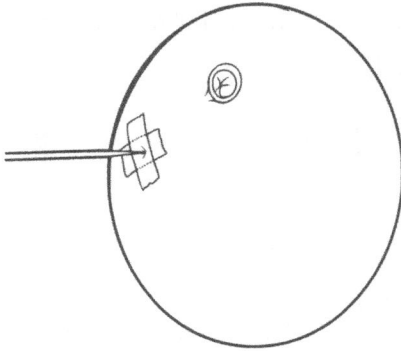

After you've inserted the skewer through the center of the first taped cross, keep pushing until you penetrate the tape cross on the opposite side of the balloon. Make sure to apply enough pressure to the skewer so that it passes through the balloon without popping it.

If you want to get really impressive, you can add more tape crosses and push multiple skewers through the balloon.

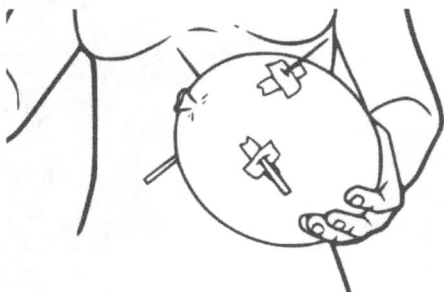

THE FOUR BURGLARS

I first read about Sid Lorraine's version of this trick in the book, *My Best* (1945, compiled and edited by J.G. Thompson). Dr. Daley created a more complicated version (*Jacob Daley's Notebooks*, 1972), which you may want to explore after mastering this easier version.

One of the best things about this simple card trick is that it provides you with the option of creating your own story to go along with the action. You can use my story as a starting point, but then use your imagination to create a different yarn to match the actions.

The Effect

Using the four Jacks in the deck, the magician spins a tale about four burglars who plan to rob a tall building. In the trick, a deck of cards stands in as the tall building. Three of the four burglars disappear into different floors of the building, while the final burglar stays on the top as a lookout. When the police appear, all the burglars make a sudden escape, magically appearing on the roof at the same time, and fly off into the night!

The Secret: While the audience thinks the trick begins with the four Jacks at the top of the deck, they don't realize that you've secretly placed three other cards on top of the Jacks. Those are the cards that disappear into the deck; the Jacks never leave the top of the stack. (You can use any three cards for the secret, hidden cards.)

How To Do It

Begin with four Jacks in your hand, showing the

audience the cards as you begin the story. Make sure you've carefully hidden the three secret cards. (You may need to turn your back for this, or have it already set up in your hand when you walk into the room.)

"Ladies and gentlemen, we are about to witness the daring heist of the century. Meet our four master thieves, Jack, Jack, Jack, and Jack. They have infiltrated the corporate headquarters of a rival company, each with a specific target in mind."

Place the Jacks face down on top of the deck. Again, take care not to expose the three random cards that are hiding on top of them.

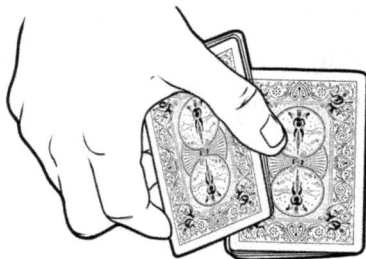

"The thieves make their way to the top floor, where one Jack stays on the roof as a lookout. Meanwhile, the other Jacks infiltrate the lower floors and begin their thieving ways."

Drawing cards from the top, insert one card into the deck near the bottom, one near the middle, and one near the top. To the audience, this will look like you have moved the three Jacks. In reality, it's your three random cards that you're moving.

"Jack number one goes to the bottom floor for office supplies. Jack number two goes to a middle floor for high-tech gadgets. And Jack number three goes to a higher floor for confidential documents. Meanwhile, the Jack on the roof keeps an eye out for the police.

Pick up the top Jack and let it scan the room for the police.

"*But, as they work, the alarm sounds. The thieves must act fast to make their escape. Using his magic powers, Jack on the roof summons his fellow thieves with a tap, returning them instantly to the roof.*"

Place the Jack back on the deck and give it a tap.

"*They come running back up to the top floor, where they make their escape.*"

When you turn over the next three cards, you'll see the Jacks have magically jumped to the top.

"*With the police in hot pursuit, the thieves jump from the rooftop onto a waiting helicopter, which whisks them away to safety.*"

Add whatever embellishment you want as the Jacks make their escape.

PAPER BALLS OVER THE HEAD

This can be a really fine comedy routine, because it puts the audience in cahoots with the magician, while the volunteer has a completely different experience. It's a good example of a *dual reality* routine, where the volunteer thinks one thing is happening, while the audience experiences something else entirely.

I first saw this trick performed by Slydini, but Dunninger did the same effect in the early 1900s with rolled up handkerchiefs. Dunninger credits magician Harry Kellar, although it's unclear who originally created the effect. I found one version ("The Whispering Trick") in a book called *Tricks With Cards* from as long ago as 1889!

The Effect

In this trick, rolled-up paper balls seem to vanish in front of a volunteer's eyes. But the audience knows the secret: the magician is actually throwing the paper balls over the volunteer's head, just out of their line of sight.

You can use different objects for this trick, like tissues or handkerchiefs. But I like to employ a roll of toilet paper. It adds a bit of low-brow humor and also creates one more area of distraction for the volunteer.

How To Do It

I've laid out the basics of the routine below. You can add to it as you see fit, making it much longer and repeating variations on the actions. But here are the primary steps:

Once you have your volunteer seated on stage, ask them to point their two index fingers at each other.

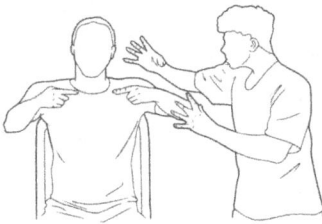

Bring out the roll of toilet paper and place it between the volunteer's fingers.

You can add comments about which way they feel the roll should be positioned, either with paper coming off the top of the roll ... or from the bottom.

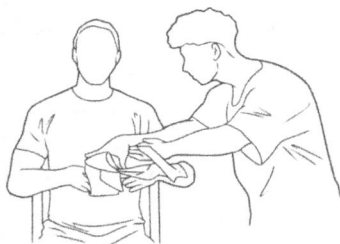

Tear off several squares and scrunch them into a ball.

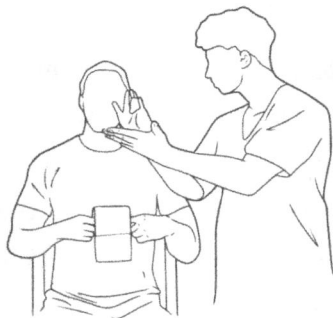

Hold the ball of paper in one hand and ask your volunteer to follow which hand it's in.

Move the piece of paper from hand to hand quickly while your volunteer tries to follow your movements.

After a few seconds, stop moving the paper ball and ask your volunteer to guess which hand it's in.

When they choose a hand, reveal its actual location, adding praise when they are correct.

Repeat the process a few times.

Finally, fake putting the ball into one hand and close your fist. Point to the hand with your other hand (which actually holds the ball). As you swing the pointing hand away, toss the ball over their head. Make sure the paper lands behind them where they can't see it.

Make eye contact with the audience, so they understand they are part of this illusion. You are partners in this hoax.

You can keep repeating the trick with variations as long as you want. Use your imagination and sense of humor to find ways to really extend this.

Explain that the problem might be that the balls of paper are too small. Suggest using a larger object and take the roll of toilet paper from the volunteer.

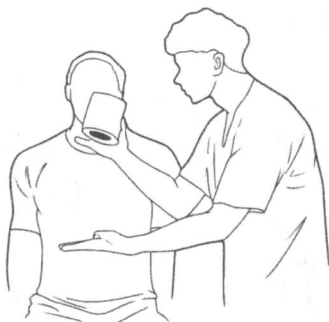

After several quick hand movements, make the roll

of toilet paper disappear just like you did with the smaller paper balls.

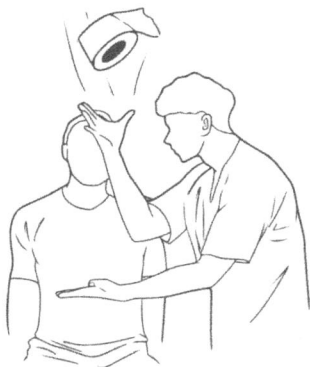

Finally, reveal the secret to the volunteer, by pointing out all the paper lying on the floor behind them. Remember to thank your volunteer and let them take a bow with you. You couldn't have done the trick without them!

GET TWO ELI MARKS SHORT STORIES – FREE!

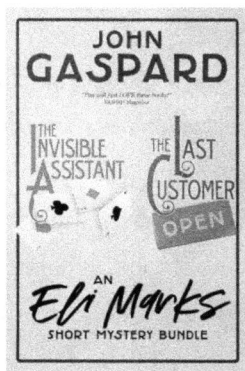

The Eli Marks Short Mystery Bundle
"The Invisible Assistant" & "The Last Customer"
Two short-story cozy mysteries in one!

"You will just LOVE these books."– VANISH Magazine

The Invisible Assistant

There's no question it was murder. But who killed whom?

What begins as a typical corporate event for magician Eli Marks turns into a twisted mystery when he is called to the site of a recent murder/suicide. Confronted by the details of the grisly crime scene, Eli must sort through the post-mortem clues - and the bickering of the officials as well as a poorly-timed allergy attack - to determine just who murdered whom.

The Last Customer

The request was a first for Eli Marks: "Can you help me make my tuba disappear?"

Magician (and magic shop owner) Eli Marks is confronted with this odd demand just before he is about to close up shop for the day. Over the next few tense minutes, he finds a solution to that question which also, fortunately, puts him the positive side of what turns out to be a life-or-death situation.

Go to www.elimarksmysteries.com

THE AMBITIOUS CARD

AN ELI MARKS MYSTERY

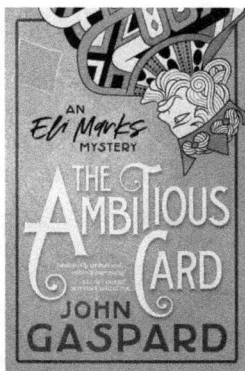

THE AMBITIOUS CARD

An Eli Marks Mystery (#1)

The life of a magician isn't all kiddie shows and card tricks. Sometimes it's murder. Especially when magician Eli Marks very publicly debunks a famed psychic, and said psychic ends up dead. The evidence, including a bloody King of Diamonds playing card (one from Eli's own Ambitious Card routine), directs the police right to Eli.

As more psychics are slain, and more King cards rise to the top, Eli can't escape suspicion. Things get really complicated when romance blooms with a beautiful psychic, and Eli discovers she's the next target for murder, and he's scheduled to die with her. Now Eli must use every trick he knows to keep them both alive and reveal the true killer.

Grab this fun and funny mystery today!

https://www.elimarksmysteries.com

LISTEN TO THE PODCAST

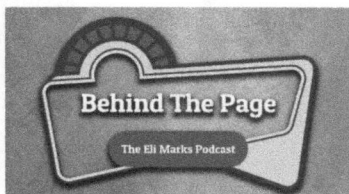

Listen to the audiobook versions of the Eli Marks mysteries ... for FREE. And learn more about the lives of magicians and performers and other ideas found in the Eli Marks series.

Each episode includes interviews with guest experts and magicians ... plus a reading of a chapter from an Eli Marks mystery. Season One presents great guests (like Dick Cavett and The Amazing Kreskin) and a full reading of the first book in the series, "The Ambitious Card."

Season Two provides a free reading of the second book in the series, "The Bullet Catch," plus great interviews.

Go to www.elimarksmysteries.com to listen!

JOIN THE NEWSLETTER

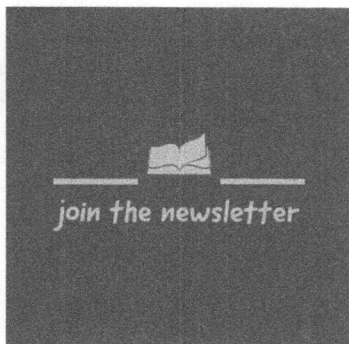

join the newsletter

Keep in touch about all the books at Albert's Bridge books — The Como Lake Players mysteries ... the Eli Marks mysteries ... plus occasional deals on other mysteries! And no spam!

Go to www.elimarksmysteries.com to join!

BOOKS BY JOHN GASPARD

DYING TO AUDITION
REHEARSED TO DEATH
AN OPENING NIGHTMARE (Novella)

Stand-Alone Novels
THE SWORD & MR. STONE
A CHRISTMAS CARL
THE GREYHOUND OF THE BASKERVILLES
THE RIPPEROLOGISTS

Filmmaking & Writing Books
THE POPCORN PRINCIPLES
FAST, CHEAP AND UNDER CONTROL
FAST, CHEAP AND WRITTEN THAT WAY
TELL THEM IT'S A DREAM SEQUENCE
WOMEN MAKE MOVIES

ABOUT THE AUTHOR

John is author of the Eli Marks mystery series as well as four other stand-alone novels, *"The Sword & Mr. Stone," "A Christmas Carl," "The Greyhound of the Baskervilles"* and *"The Ripperologists."*

He also writes the *Como Lake Players* mystery series.

In real life, John's not a magician, but he has directed six low-budget features that cost very little and made even less—that's no small trick.

He's also written books on the subject of low-budget filmmaking. Ironically, they've made more than the films. Those books (*"Fast, Cheap and Under Control"* and *"Fast, Cheap and Written That Way"*) are available in eBook, Paperback and audiobook formats.

John lives in Minnesota and shares his home with his lovely wife, several dogs, a few cats and a handful of pet allergies.

Find out more at: https://www.albertsbridgebook s.com and https://www.elimarksmysteries.com.

facebook.com/JohnGaspardAuthorPage

twitter.com/johngaspard

instagram.com/johngaspard

bookbub.com/authors/john-gaspard

www.ingramcontent.com/pod-product-compliance
Lightning Source LLC
Chambersburg PA
CBHW062124020426
42335CB00013B/1094